Morocco

Berlitz®

Morocco

Text by Neil Wilson
Revised by Robert Ullian and Dorothy Stannard
Photography: Chris Coe, pages 3, 4, 6, 8-9, 10,
12-13, 15, 17, 18, 20-21, 28-29, 34,
44, 53, 55, 56, 65, 66-67, 78-79, 85,
87, 88, 91, 93, 95, 98, 100; Jean-
Claude Viellefond, pages 5, 23, 24,
31, 33, 36, 42, 49, 60, 82; Neil
Schlecht, pages 11, 38, 72
Cover Photo: Chris Coe
Photo Editor: Naomi Zinn
Layout by Media Content Marketing, Inc.
Cartography by Raffaele Degennaro
Managing Editor: Tony Halliday

Twelfth Edition 2002

CONTACTING THE EDITORS
Every effort has been made to provide accurate information in this publication, but
changes are inevitable. The publisher cannot be responsible for any resulting loss,
inconvenience or injury. We would appreciate it if readers would call our attention to
any errors or outdated information by contacting Berlitz Publishing, PO Box 7910,
London SE1 1WE, England. Fax: (44) 20 7403 0290;
e-mail: berlitz@apaguide.demon.co.uk

080/212 REV

CONTENTS

● A (☞ in the text denotes a highly recommended sight

Morocco

MOROCCO AND ITS PEOPLE

Morocco is one of the world's most exotic destinations, yet it lies right at Europe's doorstep, a mere 14 km (9 miles) south of Spain. It is a country of extravagant architecture and labyrinthine walled cities; of markets filled with dazzling tribal crafts and works of delicate beauty; of windsurfers on the beaches of the Atlantic coast; and hikers amid the almond blossom and waterfalls of the snow-capped High Atlas Mountains.

Everywhere the pageant of life in Morocco is accompanied by music – the pounding African rhythms heard in the *souks* of the south, or the classical Andalusian music of Meknès, Tetouan and Fès in the north that echoes the intricate, 1,000-year-old traditions of Moorish Spain. Dine by candlelight in former palaces while being serenaded by soft, trance-like Gnaoua music (brought to Morocco from Guinea centuries ago); walk through the exquisite gardens of the Mamounia Hotel in Marrakesh before twilight, and you'll find them filled with birdsong.

Morocco is often intensely beautiful. If you travel to the great fortress kasbahs of Southern Morocco, or wander through the intricate medinas of Fès, Marrakesh or Meknès, you'll encounter of a way of life that has barely changed for centuries.

Morocco lies at the northwestern corner of the African continent, facing Europe across the narrow Strait of Gibraltar. It stretches for roughly 2,000 km (1,240 miles) from the Mediterranean coast at Tangier to the sands of the Sahara. The country is dominated by the High and Middle Atlas Mountains, a series of parallel ranges that run south-west from the Algerian border to the Atlantic coast, isolating the coastal plain from the rest of Africa. Its physical isolation is one reason why Morocco was the only part of North Africa to remain uncolonised until the 20th century.

The landscapes of Morocco are extremely varied. The jagged limestone peaks of the Rif Mountains to the southeast of Tangier give way to the cultivated coastal plains between Rabat and Casablanca and the foothills of the Atlas Mountains. These mountains lack any really spectacular peaks, forming instead a series of long ridges, reaching a height of 4,167 m (13,670 ft) in Djebel Toubkal, the highest point in North Africa. South of the Atlas, the landscape is dry and desolate, as befits the fringes of the Sahara, but enlivened with colourful rock outcrops and the green splashes of date palm oases and pockets of terrace farming.

As with the landscape, so with the climate. The coast from Tangier to Agadir is governed by a temperate climate, averaging about 15°C (60°F) in winter and 25°C (75°F) in summer; rainfall is

On the road in Morocco: tending sheep near Goulimine in the south.

concentrated in the north, and falls mainly in winter; the southern beach resort of Agadir can boast as much as 300 days of sunshine a year. The inland cities of Fès and Meknès are slightly cooler in winter and brutally hot in summer, but it is in the mountains that the most extreme variations are to be found. On the summit ridges of the Atlas, temperatures can plummet to around -20°C (-8°F) in midwinter, and soar to over 40°C (105°F) in summer when the desert winds blow up from the east.

Today there are some 29 million Moroccans, descendants of aboriginal Berbers as well as of the Arabs who invaded the region in the seventh century. Although in many parts of the country, these two peoples have blended together, there are still full-blooded Berbers in the remote mountain areas, where a quarter of the population speak only the native Berber tongue. Berbers can be quite different in appearance from Arab Moroccans, with pale skin, blue or green-coloured eyes and brown or reddish hair. Added to this mix are the descendants of hundreds of thousands of Muslims and Jews who fled to Morocco from El Andalus (Andalusia) in southern Spain at the time of the Christian re-conquest in the 14th and 15th centuries. In the far south you will also meet the Tuareg, nomadic tribesmen of the Sahara, often identified by their dark skins and dark blue robes. This huge and varied country is unified by Islam, the national religion, headed by the king, Mohammed VI, who is the spiritual leader of the community.

Everyday life takes locals past ancient monuments such as Hassan Tower in Rabat.

Moroccans are friendly, welcoming, and proud of their heritage – don't be discouraged by the touts and hustlers who often hang around the more popular tourist attractions.

Throughout the country you will encounter genuine hospitality and a real interest in your travels. You will often be offered a glass of mint tea – a long-established custom and a sign of friendship. You'll be asked where you come from and where you are going, and much pleasure will be taken in answering questions about the city or village, its crafts and its customs.

Far too many visitors miss out on the real exoticism of Morocco by sticking to the main package-holiday stop of Agadir. Explore a little farther afield and you will be rewarded with experiences as amazing as those in more distant destinations such as Thailand or Nepal. As you will find out, the true magic of Morocco reveals itself only to the traveller with a sense of adventure.

Break away from the traditional tourist-oriented sites in Morocco: you will find adventure and a warm welcome.

A BRIEF HISTORY

Morocco is a vast and varied territory that was only relatively recently united into a modern nation state. Its long history records a struggle for ascendancy between the Berber tribes of the mountains and the Arabs of the plains, the rise and fall of powerful dynasties, the creation and collapse of mighty empires, and, from the 18th century, manipulation and exploitation by European powers seeking to expand their empires.

The First Settlers

The ancient Greeks called this land the country of Atlas, after the Titan who was condemned by Zeus to bear the heavens upon his shoulders. Here, at the western extremity of their world, where the chariot of the sun god Helios vanished over the horizon each night and the Hesperides, or Daughters of Evening, tended their magical garden, Atlas watched over his huge herds of sheep and cattle. According to legend, the hero Perseus showed him the head of the Gorgon Medusa to punish

Berber women's dress is basically the same now as it was in the third century BC.

him for being inhospitable, and Atlas was transformed into the mountain range that still bears his name.

The Phoenicians were the first to explore this far western land, setting up a trading post at Liks (Lixus) on the Moroccan coast around 1000 BC. In the succeeding centuries they and their descendants, the Carthaginians (whose home city was near modern Tunis), founded outposts at Tangier and Essaouira, while also building a town at the site of present-day Rabat. Greek traders called the fierce inhabitants of the interior *barbaroi*, meaning "not of our people", a name

persisted through the ages as "Berber" (the English word "barbarian" has the same root.)

The origins of the Berbers remain a mystery. Some theories link them with the Celts, the Basques, and even the Canaanites, but it's far more likely that they are descendants of the Neolithic Capsian culture, which spread through North Africa in the fifth and sixth millennia BC. Berbers have preserved their own languages and traditional customs to the present day.

All through the third and fourth centuries BC., Berber kingdoms were established in many parts of Morocco. From these small strongholds, over 1,000 years later, the Berber people were to build mighty empires that ruled all of North Africa and most of Spain. First, however, came the Romans.

Roman Morocco

After the ancient city of Carthage (near modern Tunis) fell to Rome in 146 BC, the North African coast to the west was added to the Roman Empire as the provinces of Numidia (roughly modern Algeria) and Mauretania (modern Morocco). From 25 BC–AD 23 Mauretania was ruled by Juba II, a handsome young Berber king installed by the Emperor Augustus. A fine scholar, Juba was educated in Rome and made journeys to countries as far away as Arabia to gather material for the many books he wrote. His wife, Cleopatra Selene, was the daughter of Mark Antony and Cleopatra. A fine bronze statue of Juba II, found at the site of Volubilis, which may have served as Juba's capital, is on display at the Archaeological Museum in Rabat. The Romans cultivated the city of Sala Colonia (modern Chellah) at the site of present-day Rabat. The Roman Empire made few deep inroads into Morocco, so the language and culture of the mountain Berbers were little affected by Roman civilisation. Carthaginian refugees probably fled to this region at the fringe of Roman control.

These artifacts, and the kelim lying beneath them, are products of the ancient Berber culture.

The Muslim Conquest

The seventh century saw the rise of Islam in Arabia. In the early years believers were organised into a small, close-knit community headed by the Prophet Mohammed himself. Within a century of Mohammed's death in AD 632, Muslim armies had conquered the whole of the Middle East, including Persia (Iran), all of North Africa and parts of Spain and France.

Arab general Oqba ibn Nafi founded the holy city of Kairouan in Tunisia in 670. From Kairouan, in 683, Oqba led his raiding armies all the way to the Atlantic coast of Morocco. He named the land *Al Maghrib al-Aksa,* Arabic for "the farthest west". This remains Morocco's name in Arabic to this day.

The native Berbers embraced Islam with enthusiasm and joined the Muslim armies, crossing the Strait of Gibraltar to carry the banner of Islam into Spain and southern France.

For the next six centuries, the Islamic civilisation of Spain and Morocco outshone anything in Christian Europe.

But the political history of Morocco from the time of the Muslim Conquest is a tale of dynasty succeeding dynasty. After consolidating power, subduing enemies, and building monumental cities, mosques, and palaces, each successive

The Moroccan Mosaic

Morocco's 2,000-year-old Jewish community has been a small but important contributor to the nation's mosaic of cultural traditions. Numbering 300,000 in 1950, the Jews of Morocco trace their roots back to refugees fleeing the Judean rebellions against Rome in AD 70 and 135; Berber tribes converted to Judaism in the centuries before the rise of Islam; and Spanish Jews, exiled by the edicts of Ferdinand and Isabella in 1492. Until the early 20th century, Moroccan Jews were required to live in *mellahs*, or special quarters established in every major city and town, where their activities were restricted, but also protected. They established high standards in many professions, ranging from medicine to silver-smithing. Maimonides, the 12th-century philosopher and physician to the court of Saladin in Egypt, grew up in Fès, and received his education there; Britain's Benjamin Disraeli and Lesley Hore-Belisha were descendants of Jewish families from Essaouira.

Saved during World War II by Mohammed V, who used delay and non-cooperation with Vichy authorities to prevent the deportation of Morocco's Jewish community to Nazi death camps in Europe, the majority of Moroccan Jews emigrated to Israel and France after 1956. The Moroccan government maintains a policy that permits Moroccan Jews and their descendants to return to Morocco, as tourists or on a permanent basis. Thousands of former Moroccan Jews return each year, on holiday and for business.

16

Past and present meet as children scramble over the ruins at Volubilis: nearby Moulay Idriss looms behind.

regime slid into decadence, leading to weak government, political chaos, and bitter fighting, until a new faction stepped in to fill the power vacuum.

The Idrissids

Moulay Idriss, a descendant of the Prophet Mohammed, arrived in Volubilis in 788 and was proclaimed king by the chief of the local Berber tribes. As a descendant of the Prophet, he possessed great *baraka* (divine blessing), which was believed to bring good fortune to his followers. Consequently his power and influence grew rapidly.

Alarmed by the growing influence of Idriss, Harun al Rashid, the powerful Caliph of Baghdad, dispatched an

assassin with a vial of poison to quietly murder his distant rival. Moulay Idriss was buried near the city of Volubilis, and the village that contains his tomb (and still bears his name) is one of the most sacred shrines in all Morocco.

The King's son, Moulay Idriss II, founded an impressive capital for the Idrissid Empire at Fès, not far from the Roman city of Volubilis. His city was built around the area now occupied by the great Karaouine Mosque; its population was swelled by refugees fleeing from political upheavals in the great Islamic cities of Kairouan in Tunisia and Córdoba in Spain. Idriss II died in 828, and his empire was split among his eight sons. This led to a weakening of the state and paved the way for a new regime.

These columns at Volubilis have been standing tall for over a thousand years.

The Almoravids

The next Moroccan dynasty had its origins among the Berber tribes of the desert regions. A young Muslim religious student named Abdallah ibn Yasin moved south from the region of Agadir to preach to the Berbers and soon emerged as a spirited and vigorous leader. His teachings were based on the strictest discipline, and missing prayers was punished with a severe whipping. Even the Berbers, accustomed to the hardships of life in the Sahara, found Ibn Yasin's regime too harsh, and he and his band of followers were pushed south across the desert. There they built a fortified monastery (in Arabic, a *ribat*) on the sub-Saharan coast in Mauritania, and created a community of religious warriors similar to the Christian Knights of the Crusades.

Between 1054 and 1059 a small army of these puritans swept northward and conquered southern Morocco, wrecking drinking places, smashing musical instruments and imposing their strict religious code. In 1056 they took Taroudannt, and in 1062 founded the city of Marrakesh as their capital.

Despite their violent fanaticism, the Almoravids initiated a golden age of Moroccan art and culture. In 1086 the dynasty received a plea for help from the Muslim kingdoms of Spain, who were under attack from Christian armies. The Almoravids flooded into Spain under the leadership of Yusuf ibn Tashfin, who soon became the most powerful Muslim ruler in Spain and the Maghreb (the Arabic name for northwestern Africa).

Before long the Almoravids adopted the habits and appetites of dissolute but highly cultured Muslim Andalusia, and the richness of Hispano-Islamic art and architecture spread throughout Morocco, especially in Yusuf's southern stronghold of Marrakesh, which took over from Fès as the principal city of Morocco. Though Fès lost its primacy, the Almoravids graced it with the splendid Karaouine Mosque.

The Almohads

Yusuf ibn Tashfin died in 1107. Some years later a Moroccan theological student travelled east to visit the prestigious

Muslim colleges of the Arabian heartland. Fired with religious fervour, Mohammed ibn Tumart returned to Morocco and a new puritanical sect known as the Almohads, or "Unitarians", who also banned luxuries such as musical instruments.

Ibn Tumart was a religious fanatic who soon made himself very unpopular with local officials, but he acquired a large following of religious zealots. Together they imitated the example of the earlier Almoravids and withdrew to a fortress-monastery at Tin Mal, in the High Atlas mountains between Marrakesh and Taroudannt.

Ibn Tumart died in 1130 but his right-hand man, Abd el Moumen, carried on the crusade. Abd el Moumen was more warrior than preacher, however, and he proved to be an outstanding general. In two campaigns between 1151 and 1159 he displaced the Almoravids and seized control of the whole of North Africa, eventually taking over Muslim Spain as well. The Almohad Empire lasted for over a century, and during the reign of Yacoub el Mansour ("the Conqueror", grandson of Abd el Moumen), it brought Moroccan power and civilisation to a peak. Almohad rule extended from Morocco to Algeria, Tunisia, and part of Libya, as well as deep into Spain.

The Moorish culture of Andalusia seduced the Almohads as it had the Almoravids; some of the most beautiful monuments of Islamic art were created under Almohads. The influence of Spanish Muslim art can be found in the masterpieces of Almohad architecture in Morocco – for example, the Koutoubia Minaret in Marrakesh and the Hassan Tower and Oudaia Kasbah Gate in Rabat. Eventually, the power of the Almohad

Tin Mal, a place for Ibn Tumart to worship far from the angry crowd.

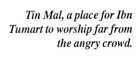

rulers weakened and anarchy reigned in Marrakesh, as warring clans battled for control of territory.

The Merinids

Another Berber dynasty, the Beni Merin, seized power in Fès in 1248. Their motive was not religious zeal, but greed for land, power, and riches. By the time they took Marrakesh in 1269, the whole country had fallen under their sway. A hundred years of Merinid rule brought glory to Fès, just as Almohad rule had to Marrakesh. To embellish their imperial capital, the Merinids constructed the "new" city of Fès el Jedid, and built the two most exquisite *medersas* (religious colleges) in the old city, the el Attarine (1325) and the Bou Inania (1355). The tombs of the Merinid kings, in ruins today, still dominate Fès from a nearby hill. In Rabat, the massive Chellah was the Merinids' fortified cemetery, and the magnificent Alhambra Palace in Granada, Spain, was built during their reign.

The demise of the Merinids in the 15th century saw the end of Berber domination of Morocco. The power of the Christian princes grew as their wealth and scientific knowledge increased. Christian warships and pirates attacked the Moroccan coasts. By the early 1500s, Portugal held most of the important towns along the Atlantic coast of Morocco, and later in the century the Spaniards took over Sebta (Ceuta).

The Saadians

The Saadi dynasty was a clan of Arab origin descended from the Prophet Mohammed. They surged northward from their homeland in the Draa valley to confront the Christian invaders. They took Agadir from the Portuguese in 1541, and by 1576 had installed themselves in Fès as the new rulers of Morocco. In 1578 they defeated the Portuguese in the Battle of the Three Kings and extended their empire south to Timbuktu in Mali, where they traded in gold, sugar, and slaves. Marrakesh was their favoured city, and under King Ahmed el Mansour (1578–1603), they lavished enormous wealth on such monuments as the palace of El Badi and the exquisite Saadian Tombs. Following the death of King Ahmed in 1603, the dynasty fragmented and the great age of medieval Moroccan independence was past. The early 17th century found the Saadians reposing peacefully in the glorious tombs they had built for themselves in Marrakesh.

Moulay Ismaïl's tomb still draws visitors (some of whom are probably his descendants).

The Alaouites

A new national leadership emerged with the Alaouite dynasty, which came from the oases of the Tafilalet, on the edge of the Sahara south of Erfoud. They were invited by the people of Fès to bring order to the country. By 1672 the Alaouites had control of Marrakesh, and the brutal but effective sultan Moulay Ismail (1672–1727) had come to power.

Moulay Ismail was a man with powerful appetites (it is said he fathered over 1,000 children) and a thirst for glory. A cruel and ruthless tyrant, Ismail nevertheless succeeded in uniting much of the country and bringing it to the atten-

The advent of the motorcar caused a plunge in Morocco's camel market, but there are still quite a few around.

tion of Europe. Forsaking the traditional imperial cities of Marrakesh and Fès, he built his own imperial city at Meknès, where he entertained foreign ambassadors in a luxury that rivalled that of Versailles.

After Moulay Ismail, Morocco again slumped into decades of anarchy and privation. Other capable Alaouite monarchs came to the throne in the late 18th century, but by that time, Europe was starting to colonise Africa, a threat emphasised by the French seizure of Algiers in 1830.

The Franco-Spanish Protectorate

Resourceful Alaouite sultans successfully played one European power against another throughout the 19th century, but

Morocco gradually became more and more dependent on French military protection, and the Treaty of Fès in 1912 made it into a Franco-Spanish Protectorate, with its capital in Rabat. The French, under the administration of Marshal Lyautey, governed the central and southern parts of the country. Spain controlled the northernmost portion with the exception of Tangier, which became an International Zone.

The Protectorate did bring some of the hallmarks of the Western world to Moroccan life – roads and railways were built, a modern education system was established, and *villes nouvelles* (new towns) were laid out alongside the old medinas (the old Arab quarters). Agriculture and mining were also encouraged. These were turbulent years, however, and for the young Moroccans growing up in the 1920s, progress was worthless without independence. The young crown prince Mohammed V of the Alaouite dynasty, who in 1927 was chosen by the French as sultan, sympathised in silence with the movement for independence, but was in no position to act.

Independence

France's hold on Morocco was weakened during World War II, and Moroccan nationalists came out in the open to form the Istiqlal (Independence) Party. Mohammed V was firmly on their side. After World War II, in an attempt to suppress Moroccan nationalism, the French exiled Mohammed V and his family to Corsica and then Madagascar. This plan backfired because it made the sultan a popular symbol of courage and resistance to foreign rule. By 1955 the French were forced to recall Mohammed V from exile. He returned a hero; in March 1956, independence was granted and Morocco was once again united under the independent rule of an Alaouite king.

Mohammed V had just embarked upon his ambitious plans for progress and development when he died in 1961,

Historical Landmarks

c. 1,000 B.C.	Phoenician sailors build trading posts along the coast.
146 B.C.	Carthage falls to Rome. Northern Morocco included in province of Mauretania.
3rd–f4th c. A.D.	Roman Empire withdraws from Morocco.
683	Muslim conquest under Oqba ibn Nafi.
711	The Moors launch their conquest of Spain.
788–926	Idrissid dynasty: Moulay Idriss II founds Fès.
1062–1147	Almoravid dynasty: Marrakesh founded in 1102 by Yusuf ibn Tashfin.
1147	Almohad armies take Fès and Marrakesh.
1130–1269	Almohad dynasty. Almohad Empire includes Morocco, Algeria, Tunisia, Libya, and Spain.
1244–1398	Merinid dynasty: the last Berber dynasty.
1248	Merinids seize power in Fès; Almohads surrender at Marrakesh in 1269.
15th c.	Anarchy reigns. End of the Muslim Empire in Spain.
1548–1659	Saadian dynasty: capital at Marrakesh. Portuguese defeated at Battle of Three Kings in 1578.
1666–present	Alaouite dynasty ushers in national revival.
1672	Moulay Ismail builds his Imperial City located at Meknès.
1912	Franco-Spanish Protectorate established.
1956	Morocco granted independence.
1961	King Hassan II ascends to the throne.
1975	"Green March" into the Spanish Sahara.
1999	Sudden death of King Hassan II. His son, Mohammed VI, ascends to the throne.
2002	Mohammed VI marries Salma Bennani.

after a minor operation. The nation was shocked at the untimely passing of the greatest Alaouite sovereign since Moulay Ismail. He retains a special place in the hearts of Moroccans, who regularly come to pay their respects at his mausoleum in Rabat. The main street in every town in the country is named after him.

Mohammed V's son ascended the throne as King Hassan II and introduced a new constitution declaring Morocco to be a "social, democratic and constitutional monarchy." As a result, parliamentary elections are held every six years, but power remains largely in the hands of the king. As a *sharif,* the king is also Commander of the Faithful, Morocco's religious leader.

One of the most important events of King Hassan's reign was the *Marche Verte* (Green March) of November 1975, when he led 350,000 unarmed civilians into the former Spanish colony of Western Sahara to assert Moroccan sovereignty over the region. The occupation was resisted by the guerrillas of the Popular Front for the Liberation of Saguia el Hamra and Rio de Oro (better known as the Polisario) but by 1987 Hassan had succeeded in controlling the rebels with a remarkable 2,000-km- (1,250-mile-) long defensive sand wall around the new territory. However, sovereignty over the Western Sahara has yet to be determined. A long-promised referendum among the people there has yet to take place.

Although the late King Hassan maintained Morocco's age-old traditions, he also promoted progressive policies in the fields of health, education, and economics, a course continued and developed by his son Mohammed VI, who succeeded to the throne on his father's death in 1999. Morocco is at present building, expanding, and modernising (the population has doubled in just the past 30 years), but its remarkable culture and way of life endure and continue to fascinate legions of visitors.

WHERE TO GO

Intricate medinas, unspoiled natural beauty, mysterious desert kasbahs, and endlessly fascinating souks – Morocco needs to be enjoyed at a slow pace, with ample time to investigate and wander. It would be impossible to see all that the country has to offer in a single trip, so it pays to be selective *(for highlights, see page 37)*. Topping the list for most first-time visitors are the four magnificent Imperial Cities –Fès, Meknès, Rabat, and Marrakesh. It's in these cities that the splendour of past Moroccan empires are concentrated. The independent traveller can reach them all by train or bus, but

if you plan to set off and explore south of Marrakesh, a rental car is useful *(see page 108)*.

The point of arrival for many tour groups, and for most people taking the ferry from Spain or Gibraltar, is Tangier.

TANGIER (TANGER)

Located at the northern tip of Morocco, where Africa and Europe face each other across the Strait of Gibraltar, Tangier has always held a special position in Moroccan history. The Phoenicians set up a trading post here, and later the Romans founded the town of Tingis. Succeeding centuries saw Tangier fall under Vandal, Byzantine, Arab, Moroccan, Spanish and Portuguese rule; for a brief period (1662–1684) it even be-

longed to England, as part of the dowry of the Portuguese Catherine of Braganza, the bride of Charles II. Under British rule, extensive fortifications were erected.

After the Franco-Spanish protectorate were established in 1912 *(see page 24)* the city was granted special status as an International Zone. It was governed by a commission of foreign diplomats, and this arrangement – together with the city's special privileges as a free port – attracted

A view from the edge of Africa: Tangier's port from Cap Malabata.

European and American expatriates and adventurers. Although Tangier today is as much a part of Morocco as Rabat or Marrakesh, it retains a cosmopolitan flavour quite distinct from the rest of the country. Its *souk* (marketplace) is somewhat geared to day-trippers, but the *medina* (old Arab quarter) still offers some real treasures.

During the Protectorate northern Morocco was governed by Spain, and Spanish is as widely spoken as French in Tangier and the surrounding region.

Ville Nouvelle

Like all Moroccan cities, Tangier consists of a walled medina, or old town, as well as a modern quarter built during the Protectorate, called the *Ville Nouvelle* (New Town). At the centre of the Ville Nouvelle is the **Place de France** and the tree-lined **Boulevard Pasteur**, lined with busy cafés, crowded restaurants, news-stands, banks and travel agencies. A terrace at the end of Boulevard Pasteur has a fine view of the harbour and the Spanish mainland; it's a favourite gathering-place in the evenings for tourists and locals alike.

The **Rue de la Liberté** (or Zankat el Houria), on which stands the elegant El Minzah Hotel, the leading hotel in town, leads down to the old marketplace of the **Grand Socco** and the entrance to Tangier's medina. At the edge of the medina, easily accessible from Rue du Portugal, is the **Old American Legation**, a building given to the Americans by Sultan Moulay Slimane (whose government was the first in the world to recognise American independence in 1776); the legation is now a small historical museum with guided tours. The Grand Socco is now the terminus for city buses and has a large taxi rank. There are city beaches, but the beaches outside town, accessible by car or taxi, are cleaner and more tranquil.

The Medina

Tangier's medina is a maze of narrow streets on the hillside above the harbour. The **Rue es-Siaghin** (or Silversmiths' Street) leads downhill from the Grand Socco to the Petit Socco; side streets to the right are filled with shops of interest to tourists. The 17th-century **kasbah**, or fortified precinct, occupies the highest point in the medina, perched on a cliff-top overlooking the sea. Here the Alaouite sultan Moulay Ismail built **Dar el Makhzen**, a palace defended by the batteries of cannon that still bristle on the ramparts. Today the palace houses the Museum of Moroccan Arts, containing treasures such as illuminated Korans, fine textiles, wood and metal work, Berber carpets, jewellery, and ceramics; adjacent is Tangier's Museum of Antiquities.

The old Dar el Makhzen, "house of government", is now a museum.

At the entrance to the main part of the palace is the former treasury, the Bit el Mal. Several rooms, with a balcony overlooking the *méchouar* (parade ground), house the sultan's gigantic wooden strongboxes – they were once filled with gold and gems. Cross the *méchouar* to the observation point for a spectacular view across the strait to Gibraltar and Spain. A 15-minute walk west of the kasbah, along the coast past the Stadium, brings you to **Palais Mendoub**, once a home of the late Malcolm Forbes, who housed a museum of military miniatures in part of the palace.

Five minutes further west along the coast is the delightful **Café Hafa** (open daylight hours), situated halfway down a cliff with marvellous vistas overlooking the sea. For decades, it has been a popular meeting point point for literary and expatriate circles in Tangier. Another atmospheric spot for tea is the terrace of the old **Hotel Continental** overlooking the port; the cavernous, hassle-free Moroccan crafts bazaar inside the hotel has reasonable prices and a vast selection.

Excursions from Tangier

Asilah and Lixus

Along the road to Rabat, 45 km (28 miles) south of Tangier, lies the charming town of **Asilah**. Just off the main coastal road, Asilah is a white-walled Atlantic fishing port, complete with an impressive kasbah. In July the town hosts an international music festival, considered one of the highlights of the cultural year.

Asilah was captured in 1471 by the Portuguese, who built the impressive walls and bastions that enclose the medina. Spanish occupation followed, and it was not until the end of the 17th century that Sultan Moulay Ismail recaptured the town for Morocco. At the beginning of the 20th century Asilah was the stronghold of a brigand named Raissouli, notorious for kidnapping foreigners and holding them for

A view over Asilah's sturdy ramparts, built by the Portuguese in the 15th century.

Hillside planted with olive trees near the town of Chaouen in the Rif Mountains.

ransom. At the height of his power, Rassouli built a palace within the kasbah walls, overlooking the sea. He is said to have forced criminals to fling themselves from the top windows on to the rocks 30 metres (100 ft) below. The palace is open during the annual festival and is occasionally used as an exhibition space the rest of the year.

The medina of Asilah is delightful and easy to explore independently. Enter at Bâb el Kasbah in the medina's northern wall and continue on the straight road past the great mosque and government offices; then turn right, cross the large plaza and continue right to the small main street of surprisingly good craft and antiquities shops. Colourful painted murals adorn the walls of a number of houses; the parapet at the southeastern tip of the medina overlooks the sea and provides wonderful vistas of the town.

Just outside Bâb el Kasbah, Casa Pepe heads the list of pleasant restaurants serving fresh seafood; it's a good place for a lunch break. North of the harbour, and the construction site of a new marina, Asilah's splendid beach stretches for miles.

Another 38 km (24 miles) south of Asilah lie the ruins of ancient Lixus. The first settlement to be built here, a Phoenician trading post, may have been established as early as the 11th century BC. It was an important centre for the Roman province of Mauretania Tingitana, and it grew rich shipping salt and fish to the capital city of Tingis (Tangier). The remains of the fish-salting factories are right down by the highway. Several temples, baths, and a theatre make up the acropolis at the top of the hill.

Chaouen

High in the Rif Mountains 120 km (75 miles) from Tangier, Chaouen (alternate spellings include Chechaouen, Chefchaouen, and Xaouen) was founded in 1471 by Muslim and Jewish refugees fleeing the Christian reconquest of Spain. Until the Spanish arrived in 1920, this remote mountain stronghold had been closed to the world for centuries – only two Europeans (in disguise) ever succeeded in reaching it and leaving undetected to tell the tale. Reputedly, the Spanish discovered a community of Jews descended from early refugee settlers speaking 10th-century Castilian.

Despite the fact that it is an increasingly popular destination for tourists, the whitewashed town still possesses an air of mystery – a 500-year-old piece of Moorish Andalusia hidden in the Rif countryside.

The main square in the medina is **Place Outa el Hammam**, lined with cafés. On one side is the ancient kasbah, recently re-stored, its walls enclosing a small museum and tranquil garden. In keeping with the town's otherworldliness, the pre-dawn call to prayer in Chaouen is a soft choir of voices that echoes against the surrounding mountains. Information about hikes as well as

easy walks in the area, with or without guides, can be obtained at the many simple *pensiones* and hotels in Chaouen.

RABAT

The capital city of modern Morocco lies at the mouth of the Bou Regreg river. The site was probably occupied by Phoenicians as early as the eighth century BC., and the Romans built their southernmost port, Sala Colonia, here in the first century AD. But it was not until the 10th century that a local Berber tribe founded the city of Sale on the right bank of the river mouth, and built a *ribat* (fortified camp) on a bluff at the western extremity of the estuary's south bank.

Under the Almohads, in the 12th century, Rabat was the Imperial capital, but in later centuries it became a backwater as Fès, Meknès, and Marrakesh prospered.

In Chaouen, many women still wear the white haik characteristic of the north.

Highlights of Morocco

Atlas Mountains. Snow-capped mountain range to the south of Marrakesh provides superb trekking; the range is crossed by two scenic passes, the Tizi n'Test and Tizi n'Tichka *(see pages 74 and 75)*.

Dades and Todra gorges. These spectacular ravines on the south side of the Atlas Mountains boast some of Morocco's most impressive scenery *(see page 77)*.

Draa Valley. Stretching south from the desert outpost of Ouarzazate, this dramatic valley offers spectacular scenery, ancient *ksour* (fortified villages) and lush date-palm oases on the edge of the Sahara Desert *(see page 76)*.

Essaouira. This fortified harbour town, over 200 years old, is Morocco's most attractive coastal resort, famous for its battlements, woodworkers and wind-surfing *(see page 81)*.

Grand Mosque of Hassan II, Casablanca. The world's biggest mosque outside of Mecca. Its 210-metre- (690-ft-) high minaret is topped with a green laser beam pointing to Mecca *(see page 44)*.

Djemaa el Fna, Marrakesh. Like a scene from *The Arabian Nights*, this square provides a nightly stage for all manner of musicians, dancers, acrobats, storytellers and magicians. From the square can be seen the graceful Koutoubia Minaret, the city's most prominent landmark *(see page 67)*.

Mausoleum of Mohammed V, Rabat. This magnificently decorated monument is dedicated to the ruler who gained independence for Morocco. Opposite the mausoleum rises the 12th-century Hassan Tower, one of the architectural glories of the Almohad dynasty *(see page 40)*.

Medina of Fès el Bali. The oldest of Morocco's four Imperial Cities, a living example of a medieval town, now a World Heritage Site *(see page 54)*.

Saadian Tombs, Marrakesh. Sumptuously decorated necropolis of the Saadian dynasty, which lay hidden from the 17th century until 1917 *(see page 70)*.

Rabat's parliament building stands on the tree-lined Avenue Mohammed V, the city's central spine.

With the establishment of the Franco-Spanish Protectorate in 1912, Marshal Lyautey made Rabat the administrative capital, and when Morocco regained its full independence in 1956 the city became capital of the new kingdom.

Rabat has a relaxed, almost genteel atmosphere. **Avenue Mohammed V**, the main artery, cuts a wide and sunny swath through the town, past government buildings, banks, the railway station and the main post office. Pedestrians stroll the shady shopping arcades on either side, stopping at the busy cafés for a coffee or mint tea.

The Medina

If you follow Avenue Mohammed V northwards (turn left coming out of the railway station), you will eventually reach the entrance to Rabat's medina. Pass through the 17th-century

Andalusian wall – note the tidy municipal market on the left – and then turn right into Rue es-Souika. Although some of the shops along this street sell leather and copper items unquestionably aimed at the tourist trade, most cater to local needs. As the minaret of the Grand Mosque comes into view on the right, the street enters the roofed-over **Souk es Sebat**, which is filled with a variety of shops selling practical items and foodstuffs. Where the Souk es Sebat emerges into the daylight, turn left into the **Rue des Consuls**, the medina's main tourist street. Here you can explore shops selling jewellery, carpets, and antiques; some also have caftans and *jellabas*.

At the end of Rue des Consuls you'll see the massive and overpowering walls of the **Oudaia Kasbah**. The impressive, monumental gate to this 12th-century fortress is one of the great architectural achievements of the Almohad dynasty. The kasbah occupies the site of the original *ribat* that gave the city its name – its hilltop position is clearly a strong defensive spot. In the 18th century the sultan Moulay Ismail garrisoned a tribe of fierce Oudaia Arabs in the kasbah for just that purpose.

Today the kasbah is a residential quarter. Pass through the gate (you don't need a guide, as it is almost impossible to get lost) into the narrow main street, **Rue Djemaa**, lined with iron-studded house doors set in picturesque doorways. At the far end is an open terrace overlooking the fortifications, with a fine view over the mouth of the Bou Regreg to Rabat's sister city, Sale. From here a short flight of steps leads down to a small restaurant and café overlooking the ocean.

For a restful break, return along Rue Djemaa and turn left down the Rue Bazzo to the **Café Maure**, where tables occupy a shady terrace beneath an ancient fig tree. A door from the terrace leads directly into the kasbah's delightful **Andalusian Garden**, planted with cypress, lemon trees, datura, roses and bougainvillaea and decorated with brass cannon of 19th-century English and Spanish manufacture. A stairway climbs from the garden to a restored 17th-century palace housing the **Museum of Moroccan Arts** displaying blue and polychrome pottery, fine woodwork, and gold and silver jewellery.

On the main road downhill from the kasbah (Tarik el Marsa) is the **Musée National de l'Artisanat**, with a small display of antique furniture, rugs and ceramics. The crafts cooperative opposite, the **Ensemble Artisanal**, sells good quality modern work.

☞ The Mausoleum of Mohammed V

On the eastern edge of the new town lies the nation's monument to the king who achieved independence for Morocco in

> Non-Muslims are not permitted to enter mosques in Morocco, with the exception of the mosque at Tin Mal north of Taroudannt and the Hassan II Mosque in Casablanca.

1956. Although it was built in the 1960s, the mausoleum is a clear celebration of traditional Moroccan craftsmanship. The entrance is flanked by guards dressed as Berber warriors. Inside you will find yourself on a mezzanine balcony beneath a magnificent, carved wooden dome. On the floor below lie the sarcophagi of Mohammed V (the largest) and his two sons (Hassan II was laid to rest here in 1999). A huge bronze lamp hangs over the tombs, suspended from a ceiling that glows with rich gold ornamentation.

The mausoleum overlooks the ruins of the **Hassan Mosque**, built by the Sultan Yacoub el Mansour at the end of the 12th century (Almohad dynasty). The sultan died before the mosque was completed, and the main structure fell victim to the elements; all that remains today are the parallel ranks of stumpy columns fringed by crumbling brick walls. The huge but unfinished minaret, now called the **Hassan Tower**, has survived unscathed, and remains as a monument to Almohad architecture. The site, set high above the banks of the Bou Regreg, is superb, and the view from the terrace is impressive.

The Archaeological Museum

To find Rabat's Archaeological Museum, head south on Avenue Mohammed V and pass to the left of the huge Sounna Mosque. Turn left on Rue Moulay Abd al-Aziz—the museum is the first entryway on your right. The collections cover Moroccan history from prehistoric times to the Muslim conquest, with an emphasis on the Phoenician and Roman eras. The showpiece is the Bronze Room (Salle des Bronzes), a separate building which the caretaker will unlock, containing fine bronze heads of King Juba II and Cato the Younger, the Roman statesman and philosopher, as well as some exquisite statuettes, such as the Ephebus (ivy-crowned youth) and the Rider. Other rooms contain marble sculptures, oil lamps, figurines, jewellery, coins and other finds from the archaeological sites at Sala Colonia, Lixus, and Volubilis.

The Chellah

The Roman town of Sala Colonia occupied a site that now lies just outside the walls of Rabat. Long after the decline of Rome, the Merinid sultans used the area as a cemetery for their own dead and, in the 14th century, built a wall around it. This area, known as the Chellah, is entered through a dramatic gate flanked by two octagonal towers. Inside, the overgrown gardens cover the ruins of a typical provincial Roman forum, triumphal arch, porticoed market streets and a thermal bath.

Downhill from the Roman ruins is a little grove of bamboo and banana plants. On the right-hand side, behind a whitewashed tomb, is a stone basin full of crystal-clear water. In this quiet spot, childless women come and feed hard-boiled

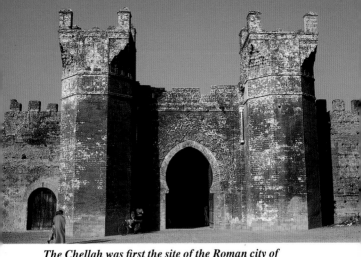

*The Chellah was first the site of the Roman city of
Sala Colonia and later a Merinid necropolis.*

eggs to the grey eels that inhabit the pond, in the hope that ancient magic will one day bring them a son or daughter.

For a few dirhams, a guide will show you around the ruined mosque next to the pond—its graceful minaret is crowned with the untidy nests of migratory storks—and the neighbouring *medersa* (religious school), where traces of tilework on the arches and doorways testify to its former opulence. These structures were built for holy men who were encouraged to pray and study beside the royal necropolis.

Sale

The Chellah looks across the Bou Regreg to Rabat's sister city on the far bank of the river. Sale was founded in the 11th century and flourished as a trading centre in medieval times, reaching its height in the 14th century. Today, however, it is merely a suburb of Rabat. Its past glories are recalled by several fine mosques and medersas, as well as the impressive defensive walls.

The bridge across the Bou Regreg below the Hassan Tower leads to the **Bâb el Mrisa**. Enter the gate and wander through the *mellah,* or old Jewish quarter, to the souks that form the centre of the town. Chances are you won't see any other tourists, as only local people frequent these busy and colourful markets.

From the souks, the Rue de la Grande Mosquee leads to Sale's **Grand Mosque**, with a tall and imposing stone doorway at the top of a flight of steps. Although you cannot enter the mosque unless you are a Muslim, you can visit its former religious college, the **Abou el Hassan Medersa**, across the way. Knock on the door to summon the caretaker, who will show you around

> Traditionally in Islamic countries, one does not eat with the left hand, or offer it in greeting.

the deserted building. The walls are decorated with coloured hand-carved *zellij* tiles; above the tiles are carved cedar screens and delicate plaster-work, among the finest and most intricate in Morocco.

The stairway leading to the roof passes two floors of tiny rooms that would have served as lodgings for the theological students who studied here. From the top of the stairs you can see into the courtyard of the mosque next door; there is also a superb panorama of Rabat, Sale and the river from here.

You can return to Rabat by ferry. Just follow the crowds to the river below Bâb el Khebaz, where rowing boats await.

CASABLANCA

In 1515 the Portuguese built a small town on the Atlantic coast of Morocco and named it Casa Branca ("White House"). Spanish merchants settling here in the 18th century called it

Casablanca, and it remained a backwater until it was occupied by the French in 1907. Under the Protectorate it grew to become Morocco's busiest port, its most populous city and the economic and industrial capital of the kingdom, accounting for more than half of the country's industrial output. (In Arabic, the city is called Dar el Baida – "White House" –but most Moroccans refer to it as "Casa.")

The heart of modern Casablanca is **Place des Nations Unies** (formerly Place Mohammed V), where all the thoroughfares converge beneath the facade of the Hyatt Regency Hotel. At the turn of the century this was a patch of wasteland outside the medina walls; today it is a bustling conglomeration of banks, hotels, restaurants, shops and offices.

The **Old Medina** lies between Place des Nations Unies and the port, but it is much less interesting than its colourful counterparts in Fès and Marrakesh. The streets leading down to the harbour are lined with tourist shops.

Nearby, **Place des Mohammed V** (formerly Place des Nations Unies), with its grandiose public buildings, is Casablanca's administrative hub. A central fountain and gardens are surrounded by the City Hall, the law courts, the French Consulate, the Cathédrale du Sacre Coeur and the main post office, all examples of 1930s Mauresque architecture.

Casablanca's most impressive sight is without doubt the **Grand Mosque of Hassan II** (open to non-Muslims for guided tours: *see page 47*), completed in 1994 on a vast platform of reclaimed land to the west of the port. It is the world's biggest mosque outside Mecca, with a prayer hall that can accommodate up to 25,000 faithful. The building costs of over one billion dollars were raised entirely by public subscription, with all Moroccans contributing according to their means. The interior of the Hassan II Mosque is a *tour de force* of Moroccan architectural motifs and craftsmanship, amplified by the grandeur and size of the structure. A

Casablanca

0 — 500 metres
0 — 500 yards

Atlantic Ocean

N

Hassan II Mosque

Aquarium

Boulevard Sidi Mohammed Ben Abdallah

Aïn Diab

Blvd. de Tiznit

Blvd. d'el Hank

Boulevard Moulay Youssef

Parc des Expositions

Rue de l'Alma

Blvd. des Almohades

Boulevard Ziraoui

Blvd. Tahar el Alaoui

Fishing Port

Railway Station

MEDINA

Porte de Marrakech

Hyatt Regency

Blvd. Marechal Fayolle

Blvd. de Bordeaux

Blvd. M. el Hansali

Blvd. Moulay Abderrahmane

Toubkal

Royal Mansur

Marhaba

des FAR Avenue

Place des Nations Unies

Place Oued Makhazine

Blvd. Mohammed V

Av. Houmman el Fetouaki

Rue M. Smiha

Rue M. Karachi

Boulevard Ziraoui

Place de la Fraternité

Boulevard

Rue d'Alger

Blvd. de Paris

Place Mohammed V

Transatlantique

Blvd. Hassan Seghir

Blvd. d'Anfa

Rachidi

Rue Curie

City Hall

Blvd. du 11 Janvier

Av. Lalla Yacout

Place de la Victoire

Rue Barathor

Blvd. Mohammed Zerktouni

Rond Point Racine

Av. Moussa Ben Noussair

Place Oued Makhazine

B. M. Youssef

Avenue Hassan II

Washington

Blvd. Rahal el Meskini

de Strasbourg

Blvd. Camille Desmoulins

Rue Brahim Roudani

Parc de la Ligue Arabe

Rue du Ct Lamy

Rond Point Mers Sultan

Rue Hadj Amar Riffi

Blvd. de la Liberté

Blvd. Lahcen ou Ider

la Resistance

MAARIF

O.N.M.T

de Mers Sultan

Rond Point Hassan II

Avenue Abdelmoumen

Rond Point d'Europe

Blvd. de Place Lemaigre Dubreil

Blvd. Brahim Roudani

Rue Pierre Puget

Boulevard Claude Perrault

Rue de Ceuta

Rue du 2 Mars

Boulevard Omar el Idrissi

Blvd.

Blvd. Danton

Rue Tarik Ibnou Ziad

Avenue du 2 Mars

Boulevard Victor Hugo

HABBOUS

glass elevator climbs the side of the minaret (the tallest in the world) that soars more than 210 metres (700 ft) above the waves and is topped at night with a green laser beam pointing in the direction of Mecca.

West of the mosque is the coastal strip of Aïn Diab, where the city's nightlife is concentrated.

MEKNÈS

Meknès was founded in the 10th century by a Berber tribe called the Meknassa, but it was the Alaouite sultan Moulay Ismail who put the city on the map when he chose it as the site for his new capital in the late 17th century. A great admirer of France's Louis XIV, Moulay Ismail set about building an imperial city to rival the Palace of Versailles. Christian slaves and local tribesmen laboured for years to realise Ismail's grandiose plan, which comprised a complex of 24 royal palaces with mosques, barracks and ornamental gardens, surrounded by four sets of massive defensive walls. Following the death of Moulay Ismail, his massive city fell into ruin, but the 20th century brought restoration and rejuvenation.

Muslims pray five times a day: at dawn, midday, afternoon, sunset, and night. Do not photograph Muslims at prayer.

Most visitors stay in the Ville Nouvelle, where the majority of the comfortable hotels are concentrated. The Ville Nouvelle is a bit of a jumble, and lacks the order and sweeping boulevards of its neighbour to the east, Fès, but Meknès is low-keyed, and many of its residents are especially helpful to visitors. A grand panorama can be enjoyed at the four-star Hotel Transatlantique. From its hilltop vantage point you can look across the Boufekrane valley to the walls, rooftops and minarets of Meknès's medina, ranged along the heights.

The Imperial City

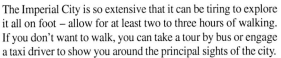

The Imperial City is so extensive that it can be tiring to explore it all on foot – allow for at least two to three hours of walking. If you don't want to walk, you can take a tour by bus or engage a taxi driver to show you around the principal sights of the city.

From Avenue Hassan II, the main avenue of the new town, a bridge crosses the valley of the Oued Boufekrane and circles the medina to arrive at Place el Hedim at the entrance to the old city, on the far side of the medina from the Ville Nouvelle. The square is a popular meeting place with fancy street lamps, fountains and a mock-Andalusian arcade housing shops and cafés.

Dominating the southern end of the square is the monumental gateway of **Bâb Mansour**, the crowning jewel of Moulay Ismail's architectural legacy. Intricately decorated with richly coloured tiles, it marks the entrance to the vast precincts of the Imperial Court. To the right of the Bâb Mansour is a smaller gate in similar style, the Bâb Jamaa en Nouar.

Museums and Attractions

All the museums and attractions in this section, with the exception of those noted below, are open daily (except Tuesday) 8.30am–11.30am and 2–4.30pm. Admission to all museums is 10dh.

Volubilis Archaeological Site. Volubilis, 30 km (19 miles) north of Meknès. Open daily 9am–sunset. Admission: 20dh (see page 51).

Grand Mosque of Hassan II. Casablanca. Guided one-hour visits daily except Friday, 9am, 10am, 11am, 2pm. Admission: adults 100dh; students and children 50dh (see page 44).

Tin Mal Mosque. near the Tisi n'Test Pass, Atlas Mountains. Open daily except Friday. Give 20dh to the guardian at end of tour (see page 74).

Pass through the Bâb Mansour and you'll find yourself on the great expanse of Place Lalla Aouda; continue through a second gate, the Bâb el Filala, to another square. The small, domed building to your right is the **Koubbet el Khiyatine**, where Ismail received foreign ambassadors. A stairway beneath the pavilion leads to subterranean vaults which are said to have served as a **prison** for the European slaves who laboured on the construction of the Imperial City. It is claimed that the underground chambers ran for over 7 km (4 miles) and that up to 40,000 slaves were incarcerated here each night in total darkness (the tiny windows were made by the French).

On the far side of the square an archway leads to the triple-arched entrance of the **Tomb of Moulay Ismail**. The doorway is magnificent (like the rest of the tomb complex it was renovated by Moulay Ismail's Alaouite descendant Mohammed V in the 1950s). From here, several elegant court-

> During the Islamic holy month of Ramadan, Muslims must refrain from eating or drinking anything during daylight hours.

yards lead to the main enclosure (grass mats at its threshold remind you to leave your shoes and proceed in stockinged feet, as the mosque-tomb is a sacred place of pilgrimage and prayer). While non-Muslims are not admitted to the inner-sanctuary they can enter the ante-chamber, which offers glimpses of the tomb. Resting beneath sumptuously decorated horseshoe arches, it is watched over by four ornate grandfather clocks, gifts to the great Ismail from King Louis XIV, whom the sultan much admired.

On leaving the tomb, take a left turn and follow the road through the left-hand arch of the **Bâb er Rih** (Gate of the Winds) to emerge into a forbidding 800-metre (875-yd)-long corridor squeezed in between two mighty walls. On the other side of the wall to the right is the **Dar el Makhzen**, or Royal

Palace (not open to visitors), where Mohammed VI stays during his visits to Meknès.

At the far end, turn right past the main entrance to the Royal Palace and continue through another gate to reach the **Dar el Ma**, also known as the Heri es Souani. This large, square, vaulted building, dating from the 17th century, served both as a granary and feed store for Moulay Ismail's vast stables, comprising 12,000 steeds. The roof of the building now supports a pleasant café-garden with a fine view of the city and the huge Aguedal Basin, once used for the irrigation of the Imperial City's agricultural estate.

The remains of Moulay Ismail's stables are attached to the granary. Nearby to the south stands the **Dar el Beida**, a thick-walled fortress. Built as a sultan's palace in the late 18th century, it now serves as a military officers' training school.

The Medina

Across Place el Hedim from the Bâb Mansour is a gate into the medina, and beside it is the door of the **Dar Jamai Museum**, the century-old private palace of a minister of state, which now houses Meknès's arts museum. The collections include wood carvings, silk embroidery, carpets from the Middle Atlas, tilework, wrought-ironwork and jewellery. The lavish architecture of the palace itself is worth seeing.

A narrow alley to the right of the Dar Jamai leads to the Grand Mosque with its elaborate entrances, ornate gates, green-tiled minaret, and red-tiled roofs and cupolas. This is the largest and most sacred of the dozens of mosques in the city.

Across the street from the mosque is the **Bou Inania Medersa**, built in the 14th century to rival the Bou Inania Medersa in Fès. The *gardien* will give you a tour of this exquisite structure. It's possible to climb to the roof for a bird's-eye view of the mosque and medina.

As you explore the labyrinth of streets in the medina, you'll encounter the mingled scents of sweet incense, tangy citrus fruit, aromatic wood from the joiners' shops, and grilling meat from the numerous food stalls. Near the Grand Mosque, huge blue doors mark the entrance to the **Kissaria el Dlala**, a souk specialising in blankets and *jellabas* (traditional kaftans). It is usually crowded (except on Fridays) with men attending the auction of blankets and garments.

Along the Rue du Souk en Nejjarin (woodworkers' souk), a number of modern stores break the solid ranks of traditional carpentry shops. Throughout the medina you'll find carpet shops housed in magnificent, once-great private mansions, worth visiting for their architecture alone.

Excursions from Meknès

Volubilis

About 30 km (19 miles) north of Meknès lies Volubilis, the former capital of the Roman province of Mauretania Tingitana and now the site of the most extensive and impressive Roman ruins in Morocco. Hire a grand taxi in Meknès to take you to both Volubilis and nearby Moulay Idriss, or if you have your own transport follow the road to Tangier for 15 km (10 miles), then turn right on a minor road. Soon the ruins will come into view, set on a triangular plateau abutting the foothills of the Zerhoun massif.

Volubilis was a flourishing Roman city from the time of Christ until the end of the third century, when the Romans began to withdraw from Morocco, but it remained an outpost of Christian culture until the Arab conquest in the seventh century. It was a rich and prosperous place, and many vestiges of its days of glory survive. From the café and open-air museum at the entrance, take the path across a bridge to the ruins. Small red arrows point the way.

After passing a number of olive-oil presses, remains of one of Volubilis's economic mainstays, you reach the **House of Orpheus**, a luxurious mansion containing mosaics of Orpheus, the Chariot of Amphitrite, and the Nine Dolphins. Beyond, a broad, paved street takes you past the Public Baths to the Forum, where the remains of the Capitol and the Basilica dominate the site. Ahead lies the massive **Triumphal Arch**, raised in honour of the Emperor Caracalla and marking the western end of the city's main street, Decumanus Maximus; ruts worn by cart wheels can still be seen in parts of the stone paving. The remains of villas lining this street contain many fine mosaics; it was here that archaeologists discovered the superb bronzes now displayed in Rabat's Archaeological Museum *(see page 41)*.

Moulay Idriss

Under 3 km (2 miles) from Volubilis, the holy town of Moulay Idriss tumbles down the slopes of its twin hills, Khiber and Tasga. In between the two peaks lies the **tomb and shrine of Moulay Idriss I**, the eighth-century founder of Morocco's first Arab dynasty. For much of the year the town is a sleepy backwater, but in September it is the focus for an annual *moussem* (holy festival), when thousands of pilgrims gather at the shrine of Morocco's first sultan. Both shrine and mosque are barred to non-Muslims, and visitors are not allowed to stay overnight in the town, but the lovely setting is reason enough to visit.

The town's main square is lined with shops and stalls selling religious artifacts, decorated candles and locally produced nougat, items that are traditionally sold in the vicinity of a tomb. The entrance to Moulay Idriss's shrine is at the far end of the square. Here, a wooden bar across the passage reiterates the following warning: "No entry to non-Muslims". One of the

The Triumphal Arch in the Roman outpost of Volubilis was built to honour the Emperor Caracalla

many unofficial guides in the square, however, will lead you up the steep alleyways of the Khiber to a well-known viewpoint, the Terrace of Sidi Abdallah el Hajjam.

Excursions Into the Middle Atlas

A number of destinations in the quiet, forested mountains of the Middle Atlas make for easy day-trips from either Meknès or Fès. **Azrou**, about 50 km (30 miles) southeast of Meknès, is known for its carpet and weaving cooperative. The European-style mountain town of **Ifrane**, just northeast of Azrou, on the Fès-Azrou road, is unlike any other town in Morocco, with expensive summer villas, built as cool, tranquil retreats from the blazing summer of the interior, and its innovatively designed Al Akhawayn University, founded in 1995. A side road from Ifrane leads to the small ski resort of **Mischliffin**, sporting two ski lifts that operate in winter when snow depths are sufficient. **Sefrou,** an ancient, small walled city 30 km (19 miles) south of Fès (one hour by bus or grand taxi), is a tranquil town, situated in the midst of cherry orchards. During the last week in June Sefrou hosts a Cherry Festival that draws visitors from all over the country for its folkloric performances. The medina is authentic and well-preserved; at its high altitude Sefrou can provide a cool day trip away from the brutally hot summer days of Fès and Meknès.

FÈS

Fès is the Florence of the Islamic World. For centuries it attracted and nourished a community of poets, musicians and intellectuals that included the great Tunisian-born historian and social commentator Ibn Khaldoun (1332–1406) and the young Moses Maimonides (1135–1204), who would later become pre-eminent in philosophy and medicine and science at the court of Sultan Saladin in Egypt. The medina – called **Fès el Bali** – is filled with fine examples of Islamic architecture and artistry. Many of the city's treasures were created by waves of artisans fleeing the Christian reconquest of El Andalus in southern Spain. The medina of Fès is among the most perfectly preserved medieval cities in the world, made more fascinating by the fact that it is not merely a historical site, but also a living city, where craftsmen, souks and a good portion of the city's population thrive in a style that has existed for over 1,000 years. Along with such international treasures as Jerusalem's Old City, Fès has been declared a World Heritage Site. A massive effort to restore and preserve the long-neglected buildings and infrastructure of the medina of Fès has been launched by the Moroccan government in cooperation with UNESCO and an international alliance of private

Fès el Bali at dusk. All roads in the old city lead to the Kairaouine Mosque and the Zaouia of Moulay Idriss II.

foundations and organisations. Many *medersas*, *fondouks* (storehouses), palaces and other structures under renovation will be only partially open during the next few years, but enough is visible to dazzle visitors. At the same time, special efforts are being made to preserve the unique way of life in Fès el Bali, so that the medina will continue to be a vital, living community.

The oldest of Morocco's four Imperial Cities, Fès is really three cities in one. Fès el Bali (Old Fès) was founded by Moulay Idriss II at the end of the eighth century. Five hundred years later, the Merinid sultans added many jewels of Hispano-Moorish architecture to the old city and built a new city, called **Fès el Jdid** (New Fès), outside the walls. Then, during the 20th century, the French built a modern city, the Ville Nouvelle, about 2km (1½ miles) to the west.

Fès: a medieval city full of modern life. Locals bridge the gap between ancient traditions and the present day.

Ville Nouvelle

Most visitors arrive first in the Ville Nouvelle, where the railway station, bus station, tourist office and most of the hotels and restaurants are concentrated. There is little to see here, but it's a pleasant place to get your bearings, plan your exploration of Fès el Bali.

The majestic, palm-lined **Avenue Hassan II** is the main axis of the modern town (tourist office on Place de la Résistance). The best cafés, restaurants and shops are to be found along **Avenue Mohammed V**. This tree-lined avenue is at its liveliest in the early evening, when the whole town turns out to promenade and sit on the café terraces.

The New Town's Avenue de la Liberté joins the Tour de Fès, an attractive ring road around the old town. At some point in your stay, it is worth taking a taxi around the Tour de Fès.

Fès El Jdid

From the tourist office on the Place de la Resistance, Boulevard Moulay Youssef leads to the open space of **Place du Commerce**, the gateway to Fès el Jdid. In the far right corner of the square a small gate marks the way into the crowded streets of the *mellah,* the old Jewish quarter. Take a stroll down the Grande Rue du Mellah, lined with shops selling household goods and food. At the far end, cross the main street, then pass through the Bâb Semmarin into **Grande Rue de Fès el Jdid**, a busy shopping thoroughfare. At the end of the street, an archway on the left leads into a high-walled enclosure. Turn right through a gate for the Avenue des Français, leading to the Bâb Boujeloud and Fès el Bali.

Fès El Bali

Many first-time visitors may want to wander with the flow of the medina (the main roads lead steadily downhill, toward the Kairouine Mosque, at the heart of Fès el Bali); others may feel more comfortable employing a guide. No matter how independent you may be, at some point, a reasonably priced guide can be useful for getting you into *medersas*, historical sites, and out-of-the-way parts of the medina, as well as for providing background information. Licensed guides can be hired from the tourist offices on Place Mohammed V or at Place de la Résistance in the Ville Nouvelle, as well as from any of the larger hotels.

> Non-Muslims are not expected to fast for Ramadan, but it is considerate not to eat or drink while walking in public during this time.

The medina of Fès is traditionally entered through the **Bâb Boujeloud**, a blue-tiled monumental gate built by the French in 1913 at the junction of Fès el Bali and Fès el Jdid. The two major arteries of the Old City – the **Talaa Seghira** (in front of you) and the **Talaa Kebira** (off slightly to your left)–lead from the Bâb Boujeloud into the depths of the medina. The beginning of the Talaa Seghira is lined with restaurants that are good for an inexpensive meal, as well as with stands selling wedges of semolina cake, flat bread and savoury snacks. For a first visit, follow the more interesting Talaa Kebira through the shaded, smoky meat and olive bazaars, and a few minutes' walk will bring you to the Bou Inania Medersa (on your right), the most beautiful of Morocco's religious buildings open to tourists.

The **Bou Inania Medersa**, a college for Koranic studies, was built in the 1350s by the Merinid Sultan Bou Inan to rival the power of the Kairouine Mosque and University. The building is one of the glories of Hispano-Moorish architecture. Intensely complex, sumptuous but orderly designs in carved cedar, hand-cut *zellij* tiles and sculpted stucco cover the walls of the courtyard. The serene proportions of the courtyard help unite the intricate decorations, reflecting belief in the unity and order underlying the complicated universe. A fountain is centred in the onyx-and-marble courtyard pavement; carved cedar screens cover the lecture alcoves in which the boys studied. The large alcove on the far side of the courtyard (toward Mecca) is a prayer hall covered by an intricate ceiling. The upper storeys comprising a network of student cells, offering views over the courtyard from their lattice-covered windows, are undergoing restoration and may be closed. If you are allowed to go upstairs, you can see the tiny rooms where the theological students once lived; the little slot next to each door was not for mail, but for the student's daily ration of flat bread. There is also a great view of the city from the rooftop.

As you leave the medersa and return to the Talaa Kebira, look up across the street and to the left. If it is not covered by the restorers' scaffolding, you will see a curious water-clock, which has not functioned for centuries. A strange and beautiful contraption of metal bowls and finely carved wood, it was one of the wonders of medieval Fès. According to some accounts, the clock chimed or sounded music to mark the hours. The clock's maker and its method of operation have unfortunately been lost.

As you proceed down the Talaa Kebira, look for old *fondouks* opening off the street. These two- to four-storey court-yards lined with small rooms once provided accommodation for travelling merchants and their caravans, but they're now generally used as workshops and storehouses by local craftsmen and guilds.

Continuing along the Talaa Kebira, at the foot of a hill, you will find the **Souk el Attarin** (the perfume or spice market). Pause here to look over the shops full of pharmaceutical, cosmetic, and herbal goods – tree bark and incense, twigs, roots, charms and potions are all on sale. Among the traditional herbalist shops are some specialising in souvenirs and Moroccan crafts. A few are set up in beautiful old mansions, and a shopping expedition here gives you the bonus of a tour through a traditional Moroccan house. Just off Souk el Attarin is the shady **Souk el Henna**, where you can buy henna leaves and powder, *kohl* for the eyes, and other traditional cosmetics.

The first side-street to the right, just before the Dar Saada restaurant, leads to the **Zaouia of Moulay Idriss II**. This structure, containing the tomb of the founder of Fès and son of the first Moroccan Arab sovereign, is the most revered sanctuary in Morocco. Entry is forbidden to non-Muslims, but you can pass the wooden bar that marks the outer limits of the *horm* (sacred area) and peer up the steps to the magnificent doors of the prayer room and the glittering chandeliers beyond

(you should refrain from taking photographs). The *zaouia* (centre of a religious brotherhood) dates back to the ninth century, but was rebuilt in the 13th and 18th centuries.

Returning to the Talaa Kebira and Souk el Attarin, you approach the richest concentration of historic buildings in Fès. This is one of the very oldest parts of the city, its foundation 1,000 years or more. The greatest architectural jewel of the quarter is the **Karaouine Mosque**. Built during the late ninth century on the orders of a woman refugee from Kairouan (in Tunisia), the mosque has been enlarged and embellished over the centuries. Today it is the most impressive structure in Fès, capable of sheltering 20,000 worshippers and dazzling in the richness and detail of its decoration.

The mosque is also the seat of the **Karaouine University**, one of the oldest universities in the world (most non-theological divisions of the university were moved to Rabat after 1956). Although non-Muslims are not allowed to enter the mosque itself, its 14 gates allow a view of the ornate doorways and a glimpse of the vast interior.

Several interesting medersas line the streets around the Karaouine Mosque. The **Medersa El Attarin** (dating from 1325), on a corner along Souk El Attarin, is smaller than its contemporary, the Bou Inania, but equally beautiful. From its roof there is a good view of the courtyard and minarets of the Karaouine Mosque.

Following the walls of the Karaouine clockwise from El Attarin, you soon pass the Misbahiya Medersa (built in 1346). The *medersa* is now semi-derelict, but it boasts a particularly pretty central fountain imported from Spain during the Saadian dynasty.

The courtyard of the Karaouine Mosque can be glimpsed through one of the mosque's 14 doorways.

Continuing around the Karaouine walls you soon find your-self in the open space of **Place es Seffarine**, the "square of the brass- and copper-workers". Just off the lower end of the square a small bridge crosses the Oued Fès (River Fès). Just before it, through a gate on the right, is the **Rue des Teinturiers**, "street of the dyers", usually strung with brightly coloured swaths of wool and cotton hanging out to dry. For a vivid look at medieval manufacturing methods, turn back sharp left from where you entered the square and head down towards another bridge. This is the **tanners' quarter**, where half-naked boy workers tread the skins in earthen vats filled with chemicals or dyes, and stack the reeking hides on to donkeys for delivery to the leather-workers' shops. The tanners' quar.ter is a true slice of medieval life.

In the Islamic world woman seldom appear in public alone; visiting Western women are al-ways treated with more respect if they are ac-companied by a man or another woman.

The bridge by the tanners' quarter is known as the **Bein El Moudoun** (which translates as "between the cities"), as it links the two oldest quarters of Fès. Cross the bridge into **Fès el Andalous**, the Andalusian quarter, and follow the main street (Rue Seftah) uphill until you reach a lofty portal at the top of a long flight of steps. This marks the entrance of the **Andalusian Mosque**, found-ed and endowed by a sister of the woman who founded the Karaouine Mosque. You will notice that it is quite different from its counterparts across the river. There is a special bold-ness in the design which seems both foreign and exotic. The main door, built by an Almohad sultan in the early 1200s, is all there is to see for most visitors, as entry is forbidden to non-Muslims. Down the street to the right of the door is the Medersa Es Sahrij, dating from 1320 and richly decorated.

A load of bright, newly-dyed wool near the Rue des Teinturiers, the "street of the dyers".

Back at the Place Seffarine, you can cross the bridge by the Rue des Teinturiers, turn right, and in a few minutes reach Place Er Rsif, where *petite taxis* can take you back to the Ville Nouvelle. Alternatively, continue to the far end of the Rue des Teinturiers and turn right into the covered passage of the Rue Cherratin, passing the Medersa es Cherratin, to reach the back of the Zaouia of Moulay Idriss II gateway. Here you will find the women's entrance to the sanctuary. The polychrome and gilt decoration of the facade is breathtaking. The copper plate below the window, covered with fancy wrought-iron work, once had a hole (now covered over) into which women could insert an arm to "catch" the saint's blessing. The saint lies at rest on the other side of the window.

Beyond the sanctuary is the **Place Nejjarine** (Square of the Joiners), the centre of Fès's cabinet- and furniture-making industry. The fountain built for the joiners, an exquisite example of Moorish decorative art, was recently restored using ancient mosaic techniques. Beside the fountain, the beautifully restored 18th-century **Fonduk Nejjarine** now contains a Museum of the Woodworking Arts of Fès. The building itself is the museum's greatest exhibit.

Follow the street to the right of the fountain, which eventually leads uphill to the Talaa Seghira, and to the Bâb Boujeloud. The **Dar Batha Museum of Moroccan Arts** is housed in a converted mansion, not far from Bâb Boujeloud. You cannot visit the Royal Palace in Fès, but the palatial 19th-century Dar Batha, surrounded by fascinating gardens, will give you some idea of how the upper classes lived a hundred years ago. The ceremonial chambers are now exhibition rooms in which you can scrutinise everything from medieval astrolabes to local carpets and costumes.

A Drive Around Fès

A good way to get an idea of the city's layout is to drive along the **Route du Tour de Fès**, a simple 16-km (10-mile) circuit that surrounds Fès el Bali and Fès el Jdid and offers vast, commanding views from the heights to the north. Alternately, take a taxi to the **Borj Nord** (North Fort), above the bus station. This 16th-century fortress now houses an outstanding collection of arms, from a 12-tonne cannon to a nine-barrelled pistol. From here there is a fine view across the rooftops of Fès el Bali, in the valley below, with the roof of the Karaouine Mosque prominent in the centre. On the hillside behind, just above the Palais Jamai Hotel are the crumbling **Merinid Tombs** dating from the last years of the Merinid Dynasty.

La Mamounia Hotel is one of the oldest and best hotels in Marrakesh. Winston Churchill liked to stay here.

MARRAKESH (MARRAKECH)

Marrakesh is the gateway to the desert, the meeting and marketplace of African, Berber, and Arab Morocco, a city of tranquillity and throbbing intensity. The city's red *pisé* (dried mud) walls rise from the red earth, glowing in the late afternoon sun; the vast souks, the best in Morocco, are filled with browsing customers; the drums of the Djemaa el Fna, the central square, summon crowds to a daily circus of fortune tellers, musicians, story-tellers, snake charmers and food vendors. Yet visitors to this fiery city can walk to the edge of the medina and find peaceful gardens, palmeries and olive groves stretching to the snow-capped Atlas Mountains in the distance.

Marrakesh's bustling Djemaa el Fna, where a meal, a story and your fortune are all available – for a reasonable price.

The fourth of Morocco's Imperial Cities, Marrakesh was founded in 1062 by Yusuf ibn Tashfin and served as the capital of the kingdom under the Almoravid and Almohad dynasties until 1269, and then again under the Saadians in the 16th century. Visiting Europeans mispronounced its name as "Marrak", and thus the city gave its name to the kingdom that came to be known as Morocco.

Today Marrakesh is the commercial centre for the High Atlas and the Moroccan Sahara, and a prime destination for

European tourists in search of winter sun. The ancient medina is flanked by the new town of **Gueliz**, a pleasant city of wide boulevards and planned urban neighbourhoods. Here you will find the more expensive cafés, modern hotels, shops and restaurants, car rental agencies, banks and airline offices. The centre of interest for visitors to Marrakesh, however, is the medina and the famous Djemaa el Fna.

Djemaa el Fna

Near the eastern end of Avenue Mohammed V stands the city's most notable landmark, the 70-metre- (230-ft) high **Koutoubia Minaret**. The finest of the three great 12th-century Almohad minarets – the others are the Giralda in Seville and the unfinished Hassan Tower in Rabat *(see page 40)* – it established the classical proportions of subsequent minarets in Morocco. Each face of the Koutoubia presents a different decorative pattern; recently restored, its exquisite, subtle ceramics can only testify to the former splendour of its decoration.

The street opposite the minaret leads into the wide open space of **Djemaa el Fna** (the "Assembly" or "Parade" of the Dead), which is probably the most animated city square in North Africa. This name hardly seems appropriate for the endless pageant of activity that unfolds here. Indeed the precise meaning of Djemaa el Fna is unclear; the name probably dates from the time when the heads of those who displeased the Almoravide or Almohad sultans were displayed in the square.

Djemaa el Fna is the heart of traditional Marrakesh. Arrive just before darkness falls, when the Koutoubia Minaret is silhouetted against a pink and crimson sky, and the crowds mill thicker than ever. You will see street entertainment at its best – bands of Berber musicians and dancers, troupes of acrobats, fire-eaters, sword-swallowers, snake-charmers, storytellers and boxers. Performers lead monkeys and lizards past stalls selling orange juice, roasted chick peas, peanuts, hard-boiled eggs, sweet fritters, kebabs and *tajines*. Around the edges of the square are scribes, travelling dentists with neat piles of pulled teeth, doctors with vials of evil-looking liquids and grinning barbers wielding their cut-throat razors. When you need to take refuge, there are plenty of cafés bordering the square, some of which have rooftop terraces offering a grandstand view of the proceedings.

The Souks

The souks of the medina spread north of the Djemaa el Fna. They are at their busiest in the early morning and late afternoon, the most interesting times to visit. A guide is not really necessary, but having one will make things easier if your time is limited. Official guides can be hired from the tourist office or any of the larger hotels.

The main entrance to the souks is at the opposite end of the square from the Koutoubia Minaret. The alley opposite the Café de France and left of the Restaurant al Fath, will take you to the **Rue Souk Smarine** – the main thoroughfare, striped with sunshine and shadow, and lined with the most expensive craft and antiques shops.

Where the street forks, take the right-hand branch. Immediately on the right, a narrow lane leads into a small square where you will find the wool market and the **apothecaries' souk**. Here, stall-holders will demonstrate the spices, roots and herbs used in medicine, magic, and cosmetics: mandrake root is used for aphrodisiacs; argan oil for massage; the mineral antimonite, finely ground, makes kohl to outline the eyes; and countless jars hold arcane objects used in magic spells.

Back on the main street, Souk el Kebir, you soon reach the **Kissarias** (covered markets) in the heart of the souk, where a variety of goods are for sale. Farther on, follow your nose to the **Souk Cherratin** (leather market), where shops are packed with jackets, bags, purses, sandals and boots.

Head toward the left through the leather souk, then turn right to reach a small open space with a domed shrine on the right. This is the 11th-century Koubba Baddiyin, the only surviving Almoravid building in the city.

The next street on the right leads along the wall of the Ben Youssef Mosque; turn left at the far end to find the inconspicuous entrance to the **Medersa Ben Youssef.** Founded in the 14th century, this school was rebuilt in Andalusian style by the Saadians in the 16th century. It is the largest *medersa* in Morocco, and the courtyard is bordered on two sides by delicate arcades, reminiscent of the Alhambra Palace in Granada. Nearby, in a beautifully restored 19th-century palace, is the **Musée de Marrakech**, displaying a collection of Islamic calligraphy and, in the former *hammam*, 18th- and 19th-century lithographs and watercolours of Morocco,

On your return to the Djemaa el Fna, keep to the right of the Kissarias, continuing through the **Souk des Babouches** (slipper market). Off to the right, use your nose again to track down the **Souk Chouari** (woodworkers' souk), where the heady scent of thuya wood and cedar perfumes the air. Turning left along Rue Souk Attarine, you soon pass the **Souk des Teinturiers**, or dyers' souk, hung with brightly coloured skeins of freshly-dyed wool. Rue Souk Attarine then merges with Souk Smarine, which leads back to the Djemaa el Fna. A less-used entrance to the souk, **Rue Mouassin**, starting from the corner of Djemaa el Fna near the Café Argana, is lined with quality craft and antiques shops with better prices than those in the Souk Smarine.

The Medina

The part of the medina that lies south of Djemaa el Fna contains a number of splendid monuments to the dynasties that once ruled Morocco. Follow the Rue du Bâb Agnaou south from Djemaa el Fna to Bâb er Rob, a huge gate in the city wall. Go left through another gate, the ancient **Bâb Agnaou**, and you will see the Mosque el Mansour ahead. To its right is the narrow entrance to the magnificent **Saadian Tombs**.

Built by Ahmed el Mansour in the 16th century, the Saadian Tombs were walled up about 100 years later by the vengeful Sultan Moulay Ismail. They lay forgotten until 1917, when French aerial photographs revealed their existence. A passageway was cut through the wall to allow tourists to admire the sumptuous pavilions where the Saadian imperial families lie buried. Most impressive is the Room of the Twelve Columns, where the tombs of Ahmed el Mansour, his son, and his grandson are marked by marble slabs.

Another walk south from Djemaa el Fna, down either the colourful rue Riad Zeitoun Kedim or the equally interesting Rue Riad Zeitoun Jedid, leads to the Place des Ferblantiers. To the left of the Place is the ruined, late 16th-century **El Badi Palace**. This was once the residence of Ahmed el Mansour, but it was systematically stripped of its wealth and largely destroyed by the jealous Moulay Ismail. Today, you will have to use your imagination to picture the opulence of the original, but the sheer scale of the place is still impressive.

Return to Place des Ferblantiers and bear right; a few minutes' walk will bring you to the **Bahia Palace**, the residence of Si Ahmed Ben Mousa, Chief Vizier to Sultan Moulay el Hassan, built at the end of the final years of the 19th century. A guide will lead you through luxurious apartments to the harem, a beautiful courtyard with separate chambers for the vizier's four wives. A garden of palms, cypress and ivy in the centre of the court is watered by fountains and adorned with a shady gazebo. The favourite of the four wives had a sumptuous apartment secluded from the others.

Medina Nights

If you opt to stay in one of the growing number of hotels set up in renovated *dars*, or traditional courtyard houses, you'll be able to immerse yourself in Moroccan décor, architecture, and the fascinating life of the medinas *(see the list of recommended hotels, page 127)*. These include the luxurious, antique-filled Maison Bleue in Fès; the elegant Maison Arabe in Marrakesh; the lovely, moderately-priced Villa Maroc and Riad al Madina in Essaouira; the inexpensive Sherazade and Gallia hotels in the heart of the medina of Marrakesh; and the simple, beautifully designed Casa Hassan in Chaouen. Many of these old medina houses have narrow, winding staircases that can be a bit difficult to climb, and rooms that depend on thick, ancient walls rather than air-conditioning for summer coolness but the staffs are knowledgeable and attentive, and the entire experience is memorable. If you'd like to rent your own fully staffed and stocked *dar* in Marrakesh, contact Marrakech Medina (102 Dar el Bacha, Tel: 44 442448), which rents out a varietiy of properties. The price for two guests in high season starts at $150 per night.

Just passing through? High Atlas towns make for interesting stops.

From the Bahia it is a short distance to **Dar Si Said** (walk north up rue Riad Zitoun el Jdid and turn right), another palace built by the same family as the Bahia, and now housing the excellent **Museum of Moroccan Arts**. The grandiose palace rooms (the reception room upstairs is particularly magnificent) are arranged around an Andalusian courtyard and display regional costumes, carpets, weaponry, metalwork, and jewellery.

Aguedal and Menara Gardens

South of the medina and the modern Royal Palace lies the **Aguedal Garden**, a vast royal pleasure garden and agricultural estate almost 3 km (2 miles) long. Water flows through the irrigation ditches, flowing between the groves of orange, lemon, fig and pomegranate trees. In the heart of the gardens is a series of huge irrigation pools, containing water brought brought from the foot of the Atlas Mountains by a system of canals. Fruit trees and flowers provide welcome shade for a quiet stroll or a picnic. (The gardens are closed when the king is in residence, usually during the winter months.)

The **Menara** is an extensive olive grove to the west of the city. At its centre is an enormous pool overlooked by a pavilion – a wonderful vantage point for gazing at the gardens and the snow-capped mountains. The pool and gardens date from the time of the Almohads, but succeeding rulers have maintained and improved them.

THE HIGH ATLAS AND THE ATLANTIC COAST

Marrakesh is the starting point for trips throughout southern Morocco. The most popular destinations are Essaouira and Agadir on the Atlantic coast, and, to the southeast, Ouarzazate on the far side of the Atlas Mountains. You can easily travel directly to Essaouira by car, CTM bus or slower local buses in two and a half to four hours, riding on a main road through gently rolling farmland. The main route to Agadir is approximately 4 hours from Marrakesh.

A more dramatic route to Agadir, with interesting stops en route, is over the Atlas Mountains via the Tizi n'Test Pass and on through Taroudannt, a walled city that is a fascinating destination in itself. Without stops, the 222-km (138-mile) drive from Marrakesh to Taroudannt should take around five hours, passing Berber villages, kasbahs, and magnificent landscapes. Take Route S501 south from Marrakesh past the village of **Asni**, which has a lively Saturday market. (A side road from Asni leads off to Imlil, the base for climbing **Djebel Toubkal**, at 4,167 metres (13,670 ft) the highest peak in the Atlas.) Thirteen kilometers (8 miles) beyond Asni on Route S501 brings you to the village of **Ouirgane**, another good base for enjoying and exploring the area. The up-market country inn, La Roserie (Tel: 44 43 91 28; fax 44 43 91 30), set amid rose gardens, offers horseback-riding, hunting and fishing facilities; the less expensive, family-run inn, Au Sanglier Qui Fume (Tel: 44 48 57 07), has been an institution for tuition for decades, and is famous for rustic French cuisine (especially its terrine of wild boar).

Beyond Ouirgane, after the road passes the village of Ijoukk, a 3-km (2-mile) track on the right leads to the beautiful, semi-ruined **Tin Mal Mosque** (built in 1153), the stronghold and spiritual centre for the acetic Almohad movement and dynasty. Dramatically situated, this is one of the few mosques open to non-Muslims and worth visiting. A 20dh tip should be given to the guardian. The **Tizi n'Test Pass**, which reaches a height of 2,092 metres (6,860 ft) above sea level, offers fabulous views of the region, but be advised that the way through the pass entails a lengthy series of hairpin bends. At the summit of the pass is a small restaurant where you can enjoy a panorama

A Moroccan Glossary

Here is a selection of common Arabic and Berber words you are likely to encounter:

aïd	holy day	**makhzen**	storehouse/ government palace
aïn	spring		
bâb	gate		
baraka	divine blessing	**méchouar**	courtyard, reception area
borj	fort		
djébel	mountain	**medersa**	religious school
fondouk	warehouse,	**medina**	old town
jellaba	long-sleeved kaftan, often with hood	**mellah**	Jewish quarter
		moulay	master
		moussem	pilgrimage/ festival
djemaa	mosque		
kasbah	fortified part of Medina	**oued**	seasonal watercourse
kissaria	covered market	**ribat**	fortified military camp
ksar	fortified village		
(pl. ksour)		**souk**	market

southward across the Souss Valley, with the ridge of the Anti-Atlas Mountains rising majestically above the haze.

The road descends quickly, passes the junction with Highway P32 and continues on easily to Taroudannt.

Taroudannt

Taroudannt, 225 km (140 miles) from Marrakesh, is an exotic walled city; it is one of Morocco's more easy-going destinations. Surrounded by olive groves, citrus orchards, and green fields, it is at the commercial hub of the Souss Valley, well watered with the melting snows of the High Atlas. At a time when all coastal towns were open to naval attack, Taroudannt's inland location and high walls made it the natural and impregnable capital of the region. It impressive fortifications, built by the Saadians during the 16th century, have been kept in good repair and provide the most striking attraction of the town to this day. Within the walls, the dusty squares and shady souks offer excellent shopping opportunities for carpets, leather goods, and Berber jewellery.

South to Ouarzazate and the Draa Valley

The other major route from Marrakesh across the High Atlas leads over the spectacular 2,260-metre (7,400-ft) **Tizi n'Tichka Pass** to the Draa Valley and the town of Ouarzazate. This pass is longer than the Tizi n'Test, but it is easier to drive and the scenery is more impressive. You'll come across stalls at every bend selling fossils and minerals, and the more enterprising boys run out to your car, offering amethysts, ammonites, geodes and other treasures. The Berber villages seem to grow out of the hollows in the hillsides, flat-roofed, low and angular, the same colour as the earth.

As you descend on the far side of the pass you feel the hot breath of the desert, and down in the valley the first *ksour* appear: fortified villages with pink mud walls, now crumbling in picturesque ruin. Finally, 204 km (128 miles) out of Marrakesh, you reach the desert town of **Ouarzazate**. A new town, Ouarzazate was built in 1928 as a garrison post on the threshold of the Sahara. It is a good place to stay overnight or base oneself while exploring the area. Today the town is best known as a desert resort and movie location; the films *Lawrence of Arabia* and *The Sheltering Sky* were shot nearby at **Ait Benhaddou**, a photogenic cluster of sandcastle-shaped *ksour*s.

The modern town of Ouarzazate is practical rather than interesting. An upmarket hotel zone lies beyond the budget hotels on the main street. However, you can hire a guide to explore the beautiful, semi-ruined kasbah of **Taourit** and its adjoining *ksar*, at the end of Avenue Mohammed V, at the edge of town. Five kilometres (3 miles) north of Ouarzazate is the Glaoui kasbah of **Tifeltout**, now renovated into a picturesque restaurant that offers Berber folk dancing and musical performances in the evenings from March to September. The way east from Ouarzazate leads along the Dades Valley to the spectacular Dades and Todra gorges, while to the south lie the beautiful Draa Valley, Zagora and, ultimately, the sands of the Sahara Desert.

From Ouarzazate to the Draa Valley

The highway south from Ouarzazate leads across barren and rocky plains before climbing over a pass and descending through spectacular stratified rock scenery to the village of **Agdz** – the northern Draa's administrative centre – with the peak of Djebel Kissane rising like a massive Bedouin tent in the background.

Here the road joins the **Draa Valley**, a wide green swath of date palms and pink mud villages squeezed between great scarps of naked yellow rock. There are impressive *ksour* at Tamnougalt, Timiderte, and Tinzoulin. The Draa is Morocco's longest river, but only after very heavy rains does it flow all the way from the slopes of the Atlas to its mouth on the Atlantic coast, near Tan Tan.

The valley narrows to a rocky defile for a short way, then opens out before reaching the oasis town of **Zagora**, lying 164 km (103 miles) from Ouarzazate. There is little to see in Zagora, but it has a number of good hotels and is a springboard for trips into the Sahara Desert and palmeries. Djebel Zagora, a black volcanic mountain, dominates the town. From here, the tarmac road continues another 98 km (61 miles) to **M'Hamid**, passing oases and *ksour* along the way. You can arrange desert excursions by Land Rover or camel at any of the main hotels.

From Ouarzazate to the Dades Valley

A good road leads east from Ouarzazate along the broad Dades Valley, with the slopes of the High Atlas on the left and the jagged desert peaks of the Anti-Atlas to the right. At Boumalne, turn left on a minor road that leads to the village of Msemrir. (If you do not have your own transport, buses or taxi rides are available from Msemrir.)

The road from the village passes through the fantastic scenery of the **Dades Gorge**. The rock strata here are nearly vertical, and have been eroded into weird fins and razorback ridges of brick red, green, and ochre. Beyond the splendid kasbah at Ait Arbi the river disappears into a narrow gorge, and the road switchbacks over a ridge to the spectacular upper valley. The valley floor is bright with almond and walnut trees and yellow-green fields of maize spread beneath the little, picturesque villages of pink mud houses. After 25 km (15 miles), the valley

*The colours of the Dades Gorge are characteristic of
Southern Morocco.*

narrows to a gorge proper and the tarmac road ends. (With a
four-wheel-drive vehicle, it is, in fact, possible to continue into
the mountains and descend into the Todra Gorge.)

Beyond Boumalne the main road climbs on to a barren
plateau, where the rocks have been burnished to an irides-
cent bronze by the relentless sun, before descending to the
administrative centre of Tinerhir, well equipped with hotels

and restaurants. A road on the far side of town leads left through a luxuriant palmery, and after some 15 km (9 miles) reaches the mouth of the **Todra Gorge**, a popular destination for travellers. This truly magnificent limestone ravine is far more impressive than that at Dades, being 300 metres (985 ft) deep but just 10 metres (32 ft) wide at its narrowest point. If you want to spend the night here, there are a few simple hotels and campsites at the head of the palmery.

Agadir

Agadir, 70 km (43 miles) west of Taroudannt, offers a complete contrast to that ancient town. Although the name comes from a 16th-century *agadir* (fortress) on a hilltop to the north, the city itself is completely new. An earthquake in 1960 levelled the old town, killing 15,000 people and leaving over 20,000 homeless. A new city, built as a holiday resort, was constructed around the curve of golden sand that lines the impressive bay.

Bold, modern architecture, wide, tree-lined avenues, open squares and pedestrian precincts contrast with the narrow, crowded streets of traditional Moroccan towns. The city's downtown revolves around the huge shopping centre of

Place du Prince Heritier Sidi Mohammed. A band of low-rise hotels separates the centre from Agadir's impressive beach. This splendid curve of fine-grained sand stretches as far as the eye can see for 10 km (6 miles) to the south and is kept meticulously clean. The surf here is fairly rough, however; swimmers should exercise caution.

Excursion from Agadir

A good two-lane highway leads south from Agadir across desolate, stony plains dotted here and there with patches of scrub and stunted trees. After about 90 km (65 miles) the landscape changes to palm trees and sand as the pink walls of **Tiznit** come into view. A fortified desert oasis, Tiznit is protected by a massive, crenellated wall. The town itself has little to offer tourists, except for the interesting little jewellers' souk, a good place to look for old Berber brooches and pins. The coast at Aglou-Plage, 17 km (10 miles) west of town, boasts a magnificent surf beach.

A scenic four-hour drive inland from Tiznit leads in roughly 110 km (68 miles) to the mountain village of **Tafraoute**. This relaxed backwater is surrounded by magnificent mountain scenery, and offers many possibilities for avid walkers and mountain-bikers (bikes can be rented in town). But Tafraoute is best known for **Les Roches Bleus**, huge painted boulders. In 1984 the Belgian artist Jean Veran covered rock outcrops in blue paint to create a giant work of art, giving a new meaning to the term "landscape painting".

Continuing south from Tiznit, you eventually reach **Goulimine**, 200 km (124 miles) from Agadir and at the very edge of the Sahara. The town was once famous for its Saturday camel market, but the arrival in the 1930s of motorised transport heralded the dawn of a new age and the end of a once-thriving camel trade.

Today, the camels are few in number, and are there mainly to be photographed by visitors arriving on bus tours. The market deals in many other local goods, however, and can be quite interesting. Apart from the colour and commotion of its market day, Goulimine has a small collection of eating places, a few shops, and an old *ksar*. In early June the *moussem* (festival) of Sidi M'Hamed Benamar attracts tribesmen from the desert. Goulimine is a gathering spot of the famous "Blue Men", Tuareg nomads whose skin takes on a blue colour from the indigo dye in their robes.

Essaouira

The road north from Agadir passes through some fine scenery, with many remote and beautiful beaches and white villages set amid groves of argan trees. The walled Atlantic port of Essaouira, 175 km (109 miles) from Marrakesh and 173 km (106 miles) north of Agadir, is one of the loveliest destinations in Morocco. In ancient times, this was Mogador, and the purple dye extracted here from local shellfish was used to create

---

Tree-Climbing Goats

The country between Agadir and Essaouira is known as Le Pays de L'Arganier, or "The Land of the Argan Tree". The argan is a relative of the olive, a twisted, tortured-looking tree whose fruit is eaten by the local goats. The goats have become adept at climbing into its branches to graze, and the local goatherds will try to get you to stop and take photos of their arboreal flocks, then request a fee of a few dirhams. Other boys will leap from the roadside in an attempt to sell bottles of argan oil, much used in Moroccan cuisine. Locals believe argan oil keeps them healthy well into old age. In the west it is gaining popularity as a cosmetic product on account of it beneficial effects on the skin.

Rome's "imperial purple". The attractive town you'll encounter today is just over 200 years old, built by Sultan Mohammed ibn Abdallah as a military port. The town plan was drawn up by a French architect who was a prisoner of the sultan, and so the streets are rather more orderly than in most Moroccan medinas. Nonetheless, the medina is filled with atmosphere. Unlike Agadir, Essaouira was not developed as a destination for tourists on package holidays. The town's frequent windy days may have saved it from excessive development.

The attractive beach stretching for miles to the south is flanked by a number of hotels and restaurants; it draws year-round European wind-surfers. At the town end of the beach is the fishing and boat-building harbour and the *skala* (gun battery), part of the old port's defences; from there you get a good view of the town walls. Near the port, from lunchtime through dinner, fishermen cook up freshly caught fish and serve them at picnic tables at inexpensive prices – you can choose your fish directly from the catch.

Beside the skala is the Marine Gate, which leads past an inner harbour lined with fish stalls to the little town square called Place Prince Moulay el Hassan, where there is a selection of attractive café-restaurants. Off to the right is the main street, lined with tidy shops and little souks. Essaouira offers some of the most romantic, moderately priced Moroccan courtyard mansions-turned-hotels in the country. The souks are famous for the carpenters' workshops, located under the ramparts, where craftsmen produce handsome furniture and exquisite smaller objects from the local, lavishly grained thuya wood.

Essaouira, bright white and windswept, is the perfect place to unwind after the intensity of Marrakesh.

WHAT TO DO

SHOPPING

The fabulous crafts of Morocco, and the souks in which they are sold, are among the country's greatest attractions. Every town and village has its souk, no matter how small: cities such as Fès and Marrakesh have entire districts crammed with souks, each one dedicated to a particular trade, while country villages have a weekly general market.

Bargaining

Bargaining is a way of life in Morocco, and although it's difficult for Westerners to live in a world without price tags (and where, if they do exist, they mean little), you need to play the game if you want to purchase the things you admire at reasonable prices.

Here are a few suggestions to help your dealings. In Morocco, bargaining is social interaction: keep a sense of humour, always be polite (so that you can return to a shop if an item you admire really cannot be found at a better price elsewhere) and, if you are really interested in buying, accept mint tea if it is offered – it enhances the friendly, slow nature of the bargaining. It never hurts to ask casually in a few shops

---

Shopping the Souks

Don't neglect to visit at least one of these interesting weekly souks during your visit:

Agadir	Sunday	**Taroudannt**	Thursday
Ifrane	Sunday		and Sunday
Moulay Idriss	Saturday	**Tinerhir**	Monday
Ouarzazate	Sunday	**Zagora**	Wednesday
Tafraoute	Wednesday		and Sunday

There are abundant open-air shopping opportunities in Morocco, either at a souk or a roadside stall.

about the opening price of an item you might consider buying, even if it isn't exactly the one you want. No two items are exactly alike, but when you find the painted mirror or kelim rug that you really like and ask the opening price, you'll at least have some idea of parameters. Never begin the bargaining process unless you find something you really want to purchase, and *never* show that you are in love with an item – always appear hesitant: "It's not exactly what I'm looking for, but about how much is this?" You do not have to raise your offer in response to each price reduction by a merchant. It never hurts to decline and politely try to leave: "I'm sorry, I just don't think I can pay more and my husband isn't feeling well, we've really got to go." Merchants hate to let an interested customer get away. Never tell a merchant your maximum price—this will then become a minimum for him.

Morocco is filled with beautiful things that would cost far more if you could find them in your home country. Remember, even if a shop in a souk claims to be a "cooperative" and have "fixed prices", this is not true. A good final price really depends on how much the merchant needs to convert some of his stock to ready cash.

If you prefer not to bargain, visit the local **Ensemble Artisanal**, a state-run organisation of crafts shops in major destinations that does has fixed prices (ask at the tourist office for the nearest one). Here you can gain some idea of the range of crafts available and the prices you can expect to pay (the variety will be greater and the final prices a little lower in the souks).

What to Buy

Architectural details. Carved panels, doors, and windows from elegant mansions and primitive Sahara villages are increasingly popular and can be shipped.

Carpets and rugs. Moroccan carpets generally have a deeper pile and a looser weave of larger knots than the more familiar Persian or Turkish ones. The finest and most expensive are those from Rabat; tribal *kelims* (flat-weave rugs) are considered by many to be the country's real forté. Although beautiful, Moroccan knotted and kelim rugs are not durable, and are best used as wall hangings, divan or bed covers, or on floors that don't receive heavy traffic. Many kelims were hung in tents or farmhouses as room dividers; the sequins sometimes sewn onto these kelims helped reflect and disperse candlelight.

Check carpet markets everywhere – there is a wide range of regional designs and specialities. Smaller shops in Marrakesh, Fès and Meknès, and the Tuesday carpet market at Khimesset, between Rabat and Meknès, are good places to find examples of older and high-quality pieces.

Inlaid bone boxes and mirror frames. Beautiful, but check carefully for odour; if the bone is not cleaned and cured properly, the item will reek and the inlay will buckle.

Jewellery. Berber jewellery made of silver, amber, and semi-precious stones is strikingly beautiful and can be found at a fraction of the price you would pay back home. Look for old, one-of-a-kind hand-engraved designs, especially Hands of Fatima, believed to ward off the evil eye. Shops in Taroudannt and Tiznit as well as Essaouira and Marrakesh have good supplies.

Hand-hammered in intricate designs, metalware makes a distinctive gift or souvenir.

Leather. Ultra soft, fine-grained Morocco leather is made from goatskin and is used for book bindings, desk sets, portfolios, wallets, gloves and many other articles. Fès is tops in this field. Leather jackets, suitcases, satchels and handbags are also popular. High-fashion leather clothing can be made to order in Agadir. Another favourite buy is a pair of traditional backless leather slippers, or *babouches*: yellow or beige are popular choices for men, and red for women.

Metalwork. Look for copper or brass trays with fine, ornate hammered designs, which, along with a small folding wooden stand, make attractive tables. Wrought-iron lanterns, mirror frames, tables with hand-carved *zellij*-tile inlaid tops, and even custom-made, contemporary designer furniture are in good supply in Marrakesh in the iron-workers' souk near Medersa Ben Youssef.

Pottery. Fès, Meknès, Sale, Safi and Marrakesh are the best places to look for good quality pottery. The classic souvenir is a conical *tajine* dish, but the choice of articles available is wide, and ranges from hand-painted plates to beautiful antique bowls and vases. Rough pottery bowls from the Atlas and Rif Mountains, usually dusty beige, are interesting objets of primitive design.

Spices and herbs. Heaps of fresh herbs and spices are on offer in the souks. Saffron is particularly cheap by Western standards. Olives, nuts and argan oil are also good buys.

The array of fresh, seasonal produce in any market is not only dazzling but wonderfully aromatic.

Woodwork. Essaouira is famous for boxes and turned containers of *thuya,* a lavishly grained, aromatic wood that grows only on the Essaouira stretch of the Atlantic coast; thuya is also made into chessboards, inlaid tables, backgammon sets and sculpture. Thuya pieces of lesser quality are available throughout Morocco. Elaborately painted wood is also a Moroccan tradition: look for ornate painted mirror frames and hanging wall shelves of all sizes. Antique boxes and chests with carved arabesque motifs and chairs and tables made from sweet-smelling cedar wood can be found in the souks of most major cities.

Special Shops to Visit

Tangier

Boutique Majid (66 Zankat el Mouahidine, Medina): antiques, old silver, tribal jewellery, and an extraordinary collection of antique embroideries, textiles, and clothing. **Madini** (14 rue Sebou in the medina or Boulevard Pasteur in the new town): world-famous perfumes for over a century. **Librairie des Colonnes** (54 Boulevard Pasteur): well stocked with books by Paul Bowles, translations of contemporary Moroccan writers, Moroccan cookbooks and hard-to-find, photographic books on Morocco. **Boutique Volubilis** (Petit Socco, Medina) offers contemporary women's clothing designed with soft, easy lines and hand-woven Moroccan textiles. **Mohammed Bakhat** (rue Nassarine, Medina) has the largest selection of quality *jellabas* and traditional Moroccan caftans.

Fès

Mohammed ben Abdeljalil (35 Talaa Seghira, Medina, next to a white arch): fine antiques and textiles in upstairs rooms. **Maison Berbere** (4 Riad Jouha, Place Sagha,

Medina): carpets and eclectic Judaica in a building that was formerly a synagogue. **Potters' Souk** (near Bâb el Ftouh, Medina): an out-of-the-way place to get Blue Fès pottery at source. **Dar Chemmaine** (off the Kissaria, near Karaouine Mosque): a student favourite for kelims. **Souk al Henna** (between Place Nejarine and Dar Saada Restaurant): traditional cosmetics, perfumes and henna patterns. **Ensemble Artisanale** (Avenue Allal Ben Abdallah, Ville Nouvelle, near the Hotel Volubulis): fixed price government-sponsored craft shop.

Marrakesh

Al Yed Gallery (66 rue El Mouasine, Medina): for quality ethnic and antique jewellery, known throughout Morocco; occasionally has Judaica. **La Maison Berbere** (23 rue El Mouasine, Medina): a decorator's dream, filled with custom-designed contemporary wrought-iron furniture, *zellij*-tile table-tops, and decorator *objets*. **Boutique Musicien** (63 Souk al Mouasine) has a large collection Berber musical instruments. **Maison du Kaftan Marocain** (65 rue Sidi el Yamani) makes kaftans to your measurements from fine textiles. **Khalid Art Gallery** (14 rue Dar el Bacha): a two-storey courtyard house selling great architectural details as well as antique furniture and textiles. **Siwa** (124 rue Dar el Basha): antique jewellery and architectural details. **Ensemble Artisanal** (Avenue Mohammed V, near the Hotel Islane) offers a good (government-sponsored) overview of local crafts. The fixed prices here give you a general idea of fair prices, and are a blessing for those who don't like negotiating in the bazaars (but by bargaining in the souks, you should do better). The **Criée Berbere** (off the main Souk Smarine) offers a maze of shops selling carpets; the nearby **Rahba Kedima Square** has interesting traditional apothecary shops, but even better Berber

Morocco's beaches offer sporting opportunities ranging from a quick dip to a friendly game of football.

apothecaries are found on the main street of the former **mellah**, or Jewish Quarter, near the El Badi Palace.

Essaouira

Galerie Frederic Damgaard (Avenue Oqba Ibn Nafiaa): quality paintings and sculpture by local artists.

SPORTS

Swimming and water sports. Morocco has 2,000 km (1,250 miles) of coastline facing the Atlantic Ocean, with several outstanding **beaches**. The best are at Agadir and Essaouira, and at Asilah, south of Tangier. It is advisable not to venture out of your depth anywhere on the Atlantic coast. If an undertow catches you it can sweep you out to sea in a matter of minutes.

Morocco's Mediterranean beaches are pleasant and varied, and generally free from the threat of undertow. Those backed by the Rif Mountains have only recently been developed as resorts and many of them are very attractive, most notably those around Al Hoceima. Explore the possibilities at Cabo Negro, Smir-Restinga, and Taïfor.

Surfing and wind-surfing have become very popular on the breezy Atlantic coast of Morocco. Tarhazoute, just north of Agadir, and Essaouira have acquired an international reputation as two of Morocco's best sites. **Sailing and scuba-diving** are available in Agadir.

Fishing. Morocco offers opportunities for deep-sea angling and rock-fishing as well as surf-casting on the Atlantic and Mediterranean coasts, and freshwater angling for trout, bass, and pike in the lakes and streams of the Atlas Mountains. All freshwater anglers require a permit from the Service des Eaux et Forets (Waters and Forests Service), which also gives out information on closed seasons and local regulations. Contact the ONMTfor details *(see page 125)*.

Golf. In Morocco, golf is a royal sport: King Hassan II was a great devotee of the game. The **Royal Dar-Es-Salam Club** at Rabat boasts one 9-hole and two 18-hole championship golf courses, designed by Robert Trent Jones, with luxurious clubhouse facilities. There are other 18-hole courses at Mohammedia, Tangier, El Jadida, and Marrakesh, and 9-hole courses at Agadir, Cabo Negro (near Tetouan), Meknès, Fès, Casablanca, and Ouarzazate. The links are open all year and green fees are reasonable. Marrakesh's five-star **Palmarie Golf Palace Hotel** (reservations from North America; Tel. 212/268-1554; fax 212/268-0958; in Morocco; Tel: 044 30 10 10; fax: 044 30 50 50) is geared to golf holidays; it's near Marrakesh's 18-hole Robert Trent Jones course.

Horseback riding. You can hire a mount in Agadir for a ride along the beach or out into the countryside, while organised treks into the High Atlas are run from the Hôtel La

The Tour de Maroc may be too gruelling for your tastes, but there are other cycling choices on offer.

Roseraie at Ouirgane, near Marrakesh. For further information, contact the ONMT *(see page 125)*.

Hunting. For enthusiasts, there's a 119,000-ha (295,000-acre) hunting reserve at Arbaoua, near the coast south of Larache, and smaller reserves near Marrakesh, Agadir, Kabila, and Benslimane. Arrangements are best made through a specialist tour operator in your home country; for details, contact the ONMT *(see page 125)*.

Winter sports. You can ski in the Atlas Mountains between December and April, snow conditions permitting. The biggest resort is **Oukaimeden**, 70 km (44 miles) south of Marrakesh, at an altitude of 3,200 metres (10,500 ft); it has a few hotels, one chair-lift and six tows, and equipment rental is available. There are smaller ski areas at **Ifrane**, near Meknès. Hotel reservations are advisable on weekends.

Trekking and mountain biking. A number of adventure holiday companies now offer trekking and mountain-biking trips in the Atlas Mountains. The High Atlas offers a good selection of high-level, multi-day walking routes, with accommodation in French Alpine Club mountain huts. In winter, the high peaks provide a challenging playground for all experienced mountaineers. The many unsurfaced roads and tracks that wind through the valleys provide ideal terrain for mountain bikers; the tour companies organise accommodations as well as provide Land Rover back-up. Contact the ONMT *(see page 125)*.

ENTERTAINMENT

Nightlife

Early evening is promenade time in all Moroccan towns, when it seems as if the entire population turns out for a stroll along the main avenue with family and friends and a chat over coffee or mint tea.

Major hotels and traditional Moroccan restaurants in the main tourist cities offer evening entertainment in the form of a Moroccan banquet, with folk music, dancing and, perhaps, a belly dancer. Some of the expensive medina restaurants in Fès and Marrakesh are in former palaces, wonderful for an extravagant, leisurely meal and worth visiting for the decor alone. By Western standards, some of the banquets at palace restaurants are not much more than dinner at a moderate restaurant at home.

In Rabat, Casablanca, Marrakesh, Tangier, and Agadir, you'll find a few European-style bars and discos. They stay open until late – ask your hotel receptionist for a recommendation. There's a casino in Marrakesh's Hotel Mamounia: dress smartly or you won't be admitted.

Folklore and Festivals

The best possible way to experience genuine Moroccan folk music and dance, away from a tourist-oriented environment, is